They Preached Liberty

An anthology of timely quotations
from New England ministers of the American
Revolution on the subject of Liberty:
Its source, nature, obligations,
types, and blessings

They Preached Liberty

With an Introductory Essay and
Biographical Sketches by
Franklin P. Cole

Liberty*Press*

Indianapolis

Liberty Press is the publishing imprint of Liberty Fund, Inc., a foundation established to encourage study of the ideal of a society of free and responsible individuals.

The cuneiform inscription that serves as the design motif for our endpapers is the earliest known written appearance of the word "freedom" *(ama-gi),* or liberty. It is taken from a clay document written about 2300 B.C. in the Sumerian city-state of Lagash.

All inquiries should be addressed to Liberty Fund, Inc., 7440 North Shadeland, Indianapolis, Indiana 46250. This book was manufactured in the United States of America.

Library of Congress Catalog Card No.: 76-26327
ISBN 0-913966-16-9

"Man will ultimately be governed
by God or by tyrants."
—*Benjamin Franklin*

Contents

They Preached Liberty

Preface

The New England ministers are "the forgotten men" among the heroes of the American Revolution. If they are pictured at all in the distorted imagination of the average citizen, they appear as witch hunters, or long-winded exponents of an archaic theology, or as vigilantes snooping into the private lives of their parishioners—a divinely ordained Colonial Gestapo.

This volume is aimed to correct, to whatever degree possible, the current misconception of their work and defamation of their character. Their sermons and writings, their devotion to education and good government, their patriotic activities during the Revolution—all testify to the fact that "there were giants in those days."

The Church today is vitally concerned with liberty. Whence does it originate? Is it a divine gift or an outmoded theory of human rationalism? What are the obligations of liberty, its types and results? The New England ministers answered these questions so wisely that their answers have contemporary significance. They preached when liberty was under fire, as it is today. While they cannot solve our problems for us, they can afford us insight and inspiration, perhaps even formulas and programs.

I wish to acknowledge the courtesy and help which I received at the Massachusetts Historical Society, the Maine Historical Society, the Rare Book Department of the Boston Public Library, and the Congregational Library of Boston. My wife, Eleanor S. Cole, and her father, Judge H. R. Snavely, have been largely responsible for the completion of this volume.

— F. P. C.

Portland, Maine

Watchmen on Liberty's Wall

By Franklin P. Cole

In his Election Sermon of 1772, before the Massachusetts Council and House of Representatives, the Rev. Moses Parsons, of Newbury Falls, stated his conception of the duty of ministers: "Watchmen upon the walls must not hold their peace—they must cry and not spare, must reprove for what is amiss, and warn when danger is approaching."

The New England minister of the Revolutionary era was a watchman on several walls. He was a guardian of education. Practically all the Puritan clergy had been educated at Harvard or Yale; the more influential of them having their Master's or Doctor's degree. In 1764, of the fifty-two settled Congregational ministers in New Hampshire, forty-eight were college graduates. The minister was usually the best educated man in his community. It was natural that his leadership should be exercised in the elementary schools of his town. He also retained his interest in higher education. In many of the Massachusetts and Connecticut Election Sermons of 1750-80, the preachers bade the legislators to "remember the college to which we are all indebted."

Contrary to popular opinion of the present day, many of the ministers of the Revolutionary period were interested in other fields of knowledge besides theology. In 1778, the Rev. Phillips Payson of Chelsea declared in his Massachusetts Election Sermon: "In matters of science we have a most ample field for improvement. To complete the geography of our country, to improve in the arts of agriculture and manufacture, and of physic, and other branches of science, are great objects that demand our special attention." Incidentally, the American Academy of Arts and Sciences was established in 1780, two years after his recommendation. Many other ministers were equally interested in broad, liberal education.

Their principal wall or fort was, of course, religion and morality. Some looking down from this wall saw a barren world and a lost humanity. Those who saw only the panorama of Calvinism did not view it through rose-colored glasses. But many, including the leading clergymen, saw and appreciated natural beauty, developing arts and sciences, ancient and modern literature, and a humanity possessing free will. Theological liberalism of the present time may well profit from many of the utterances of Jonathan Mayhew, Samuel Cooper, Simeon Howard, and Ezra Stiles. But all of them, whether theologically liberal or conservative, regarded religion as their principal stronghold. And from that wall they proclaimed the ageless gospel.

Yet, as the title and contents of this anthology suggest, the ministers were watchmen on another wall—the wall of liberty. They were as ready to sing the praises of freedom as to warn of the dangers when it was threatened. Some people in their day thought that liberty was not a wall, bearing high standards and imposing restraining influences on conduct. That is, the unthinking and irresponsible people in their day, as in ours, identified liberty with licentiousness. To the ministers this view was sacrilege. In sermon after sermon they declared (with kindred phraseology as well as thought): "We have more to fear from our own licentiousness and immorality than from the arms of our enemies." For them liberty was a wall that required a solid foundation and strong materials of morality if it was to stand. And standing, it shut out degrading influences of anarchy, and shut in justice, vigilance, and righteousness.

It was in the so-called "Election Sermons" of Massachusetts, Connecticut, New Hampshire, and Vermont that the ministers expressed themselves most fluently on the subject of civil government. According to the Rev. William Gordon of Roxbury, an historian of the Revolution: "Two sermons have been preached annually for a length of time, the one on general election day, the last Wednesday in May, when the new general court has been used to meet, according to charter, and elect counsellors for the ensuing year; the other, some little while after, on the artillery election day, when the officers are re-elected, or new officers chosen. On these occasions political subjects are deemed very proper; but it is expected that they be treated in a decent, serious, and instructive manner. . . . The sermon is styled the *Election Sermon* and is printed. Every representative has a copy for himself, and generally one or more for the minister or ministers of his town. As the patriots have prevailed, the preachers of each sermon have been the zealous friends of liberty; and the passages most adapted to promote the spread and love of it have been selected and circulated far and wide by means of newspapers.''

On other occasions, like Thanksgiving or Fast Days, or upon receiving momentous news from abroad, the ministers spoke on political subjects. The majority of their hearers must have welcomed their views and interpretations. But those who were Tories strongly objected. After William Gordon's sermon of December 15, 1776, one of the ''king's friends'' ejaculated: ''I most heartily wish, for the peace of America, that he and many others of his profession would confine themselves to gospel truths!'' (How modern the Tory sounds in his defense of the *simple* gospel.)

For the Puritan ministers the cornerstone of Liberty's Wall was the Bible. ''Where the spirit of the Lord is, there is liberty,'' was a favorite text. ''Ye shall know the truth and the truth shall make you free.'' ''Take away your exactions from my people, saith the Lord God.'' Upon these and similar declarations of the Scriptures the patriot-preachers fed their souls. They rejoiced with the Hebrew Children leaving the land of bondage and entering the Promised Land. They reveled in the historical books of the Bible, and noted that Jehovah "in his anger" gave Israel a king. They were well read in the prophetic books, and often made reference to the Babylonian Captivity. They pictured Jesus fighting the cause of religious liberty against the scribes and Pharisees. Charles Turner of Duxbury expressed the point of view of his profession: "The scriptures cannot rightly be expounded without explaining them in a manner friendly to the cause of freedom."

The ministers, as a result of their classical education, were also well grounded in the Greek and Roman authors. Plato, Aristotle, and Thucydides were frequently quoted. Latin quotations from Cicero, Vergil, Seneca, and Tacitus were not uncommon. And from the ancients they learned the fruits of both liberty and tyranny.

In their sermons on political themes they quote again and again from John Locke, "that very wise man." Likewise from Milton, Sydney, Montesquieu, Butler, and other writers on government.

From these ancient and modern authorities, and from their own thinking and experience, the New England ministers reached definite conclusions, which they shared almost unanimously.

Following a Pauline lead, Jonathan Mayhew in 1754 declared: "Rulers derive their power from God, and are ordained to be his *ministers for good*." Scarcely an Election Sermon fails to emphasize this premise. The power of

God is the source of all authority. Yet even the divine power is "restrained by the eternal laws of truth, wisdom, and equity." Human power must be restrained also by the laws of the commonwealth. No king or magistrate can claim to rule by "divine right" unless he has the lawful consent of his subjects and constantly ministers to their welfare.

The necessity of government is writ in the eternal laws. "Reason dictates that there should be government, and the voice of reason is the voice of God." But God in His wisdom did not decree the *form* of government that a particular state or society should adopt. The form should be determined by the people themselves.

The Revolutionary parsons distinguished between natural rights and civil rights. People undergoing a transition from "a state of nature" to a "society" may feel that they are losing certain fundamental liberties. But they are not losing liberty; they are guaranteeing it. The only way they can become, to say nothing of remain, a free people is through a government that makes secure "life, liberty, and property."

Both their faith and their reason led the ministers to believe in government by *compact* or *constitution*. Even God rules in accordance with the constitution of natural laws. Even God made His compact with Noah, Moses, and Joshua. If God, who rules by just laws anyway, made His compact with man, how natural and essential it is for imperfect human rulers to rule according to a constitution setting forth their duties and limiting their power. Thomas Barnard in 1763 said: "All power has its foundation in compact and mutual consent or else it proceeds from fraud or violence.'' The parsons were staunch believers in compacts, constitutions, and Magna Chartas.

Their belief in liberty was grounded in the Scriptures and their understanding of both human and divine laws. Therefore they were prepared in season and out of season to proclaim that belief as watchmen on the walls.

With the powerful New England merchants the case was different. They were conscious of their liberties only when their prosperity was threatened. The "Sugar Act" of 1764 was deeply resented by the mercantile group, not alone because of its additional duties, but also because of its partial enforcement by the British warships. It was not long, however, before smuggling became an honorable practice even for John Hancock. Discussions of liberty were purely academic so long as profit, legitimate or illegitimate, could be made. When the Townshend Acts of 1767, laying duties on tea, lead, glass, etc., were passed, the merchants were vocal in their annoyance. But when the Acts were repealed, they were prepared to bury the hatchet with England, but to wield another against Sam Adams and his confederates who were "disturbing the peace." A few years later, however, when Lord North in 1773 granted the East India Company the monopoly on the transportation of tea to America, the merchants again stood with the "hundred percent patriots." Thus in the decade preceding the Revolution economic fortune or misfortune determined for the merchant class their convictions regarding political liberty.

It would be incorrect to assume, much less to assert, that

the New England ministers were unaffected in sentiment by British colonial policy and local economic conditions. They rejoiced with the lawyers and tradesmen when the Stamp Act was repealed; in fact, practically every pulpit rang with ''the good news from a far land.'' But even on that happy occasion many parsons took the opportunity to warn against possible future infringements of colonial liberties. They were not at all sure that the ''snare,'' as Mayhew called it, had been permanently broken. Their convictions of liberty were so deeply grounded, as we noted above, that the sunshine of prosperity did not quickly warm, and the winds of adversity did not easily sway, their rock-like principles and beliefs.

The ministers before and during the Revolution stood, with few exceptions, near the center of liberty's wall. They were, as a group, neither radical nor reactionary in their political philosophy. As one would expect, there were individual differences of opinion, and even notable differences by states. For example, there were more Tory sympathizers among the clergy of Connecticut than of Massachusetts. But of the three groups named by James Truslow Adams in his *History of the United States*— namely, the ''ultra-Loyalists,'' the ''extreme radicals,'' and ''in between the vast mass of Americans who wanted above all else to be allowed to live their lives and earn their bread in peace, unmolested by new and annoying British laws or the violence of American radical mobs''—of the three groups, the ministers stood with the middle-of-the-roaders.

They could not stand with the "ultra-Loyalists," who believed that His Majesty's government could do no wrong. They knew their Pharaohs, Nebuchadnezzars, and Caesars too well! Their Pilgrim and Puritan ancestors had suffered too much persecution under the Stuarts, "that infamous race of sceptered tyrants," for the ministers to accept, willy-nilly, any theory of the divine rights of king or parliament. They gloried in the Revolution of 1688, when "God raised up a Deliverer, the Prince of Orange, afterward the glorious King William, the great Restorer of the English Constitution." Thomas Frink of Rutland, who so lauded William of Orange in his Election Sermon of 1758, continued with this declaration: "The happy Revolution ought never to be forgotten by Protestants, Britons, and Transmarine English."

While the parsons favored revolutions that had yielded or would yield fruits of human freedom, they did not stand with the "extreme radicals" who were busy stirring up mob spirit and violence. They were not anarchists or chronic revolutionists. They viewed with horror those who, without legal authority, took the law into their own hands. The ministers were Constitutionalists who believed in reasonable laws imposing obligations upon both governors and the governed. If rulers violate their compact with the people, the rulers should be voted out of office. But, said Andrew Eliot of Boston, in 1765, "when rulers are wise and good, opposition is a high crime." People should respect their rulers provided the rulers are worthy of respect.

From this point of view, the ministers may perhaps be regarded as conservative. They wished to conserve the best from the past, including Magna Charta and their own colonial charters. In their opinion, the real radicals were those in the British government who were departing from the laws and traditions of old. The clergy opposed what Samuel Langdon, D.D., the President of Harvard College, called, "the many artifices to stretch the prerogatives of the crown beyond all constitutional bounds." In that opposition to the new tyranny, they regarded themselves as defenders of the ancient liberties.

It seems superfluous in this introduction to review in any detail the declarations of the ministers on the subject of liberty. The quotations in the anthology speak for themselves. One may note that they had much to say on the divine source and the Puritan heritage of liberty. In fact, they said so much on these themes that only a few of their many sayings have been included. It will be observed how strongly, even colorfully, they express themselves on civil and religious liberty, as well as the liberty resulting from education. They speak so unanimously of the benefits of education that here again to include all their statements would seem repetitious. They did not stop, however, with a glowing picture of the blessings of liberty. Being rationalists by nature and training, they proceeded to point out the cost and obligations of liberty.

Liberty to them was not easily achieved; it involved a most delicate balance between authority of the ruler and submission of the subject; between constitutional law and the insight with which it was interpreted; and between natural rights on the one hand, and civil responsibilities on the other.

As early as 1770, the New England parsons began pleading the cause of the African slaves. In that year Samuel Cooke of Cambridge petitioned the Massachusetts Assembly for ''some effective measures, at least to prevent the future importation of them.'' And he continued: ''Let the time pass wherein we, the patrons of liberty, have dishonored the Christian name, and degraded human nature nearly to the level of the beasts that perish.'' It will be recalled that in the original draft of the Declaration of Independence, Jefferson denounced the British government for permitting slavery—a clause which the delegates from Georgia and South Carolina succeeded in striking from the Declaration. But the record of the clergy's protest against slavery may still be seen in several pre-Revolutionary War sermons.

The final section of the anthology is on ''America the Free.'' Only a few of the prophets who had so long spoken of the heritage, nature, and obligations of liberty left a record of their visions of the future free America. Some of those visions, so utopian in their day, have been remarkably fulfilled in reality.

So much for the trumpet blasts from the Wall of Liberty. Now let us glance at a few of the watchmen. The record of the lives of many whose convictions are expressed in this volume, is lost to posterity. But the stature of a few of them seems even now to be silhouetted against the American

horizon, as though they were still in a sunset hour guarding
the Wall of Liberty.

JONATHAN MAYHEW (1720-1766)

It is regrettable that Jonathan Mayhew is not better
known and more rightfully honored by our generation. For
he was an inspired, courageous pioneer, not only in his
theological thought, but also in his convictions regarding
civil and religious liberties. Robert Treat Paine, a signer of
the Declaration of Independence and one-time attorney-
general of the United States, called Mayhew "The Father
of Civil and Religious Liberty in Massachusetts and
America." John Adams not only ranked him along with
Otis and Samuel Adams as a patriot-statesman, but also
said of him: "To draw the character of Mayhew would be
to transcribe a dozen volumes."

He was born on Martha's Vineyard in 1720, the son of
the Rev. Experience and Remember Mayhew, who did
heroic missionary work among the Indians. His grandfather, Thomas Mayhew, sold Nantucket Island in 1659 to
nine purchasers for "the sum of thirty pounds in good
Merchantable Pay, . . . and two Beaver Hatts one for
myself and one for my wife."

Jonathan graduated from Harvard with honors in 1744.
In his sermon on the repeal of the Stamp Act, he speaks of
his early training: "Having been initiated in youth in the
doctrines of civil liberty, as they were taught by such men
as Plato, Demosthenes, Cicero, and other renowned
persons among the ancients; and such as Sydney and

Jonathan Mayhew

Milton, Locke and Hoadley among the moderns, I liked
them; they seemed rational. And having learnt from the
Holy Scriptures that wise, brave and virtuous men were
always friends to liberty,—that God gave the Israelites a
king in his anger, because they had not sense and virtue
enough to be a free commonwealth,—and that 'where the
spirit of the Lord is, there is liberty,'—this made me
conclude that freedom was a great blessing.''

His theology was as liberal as his politics. He defended
the right of private judgment in an authoritarian age. He
defended the reality of free will in a Calvinistic state. As
early as 1755 he rejected the doctrine of the Trinity,
finding it irrelevant. Ignoring the creeds and doctrines of
both Catholicism and Calvinism, Mayhew went directly to
the Bible for his religious authority. He was a Christian
liberal, a hundred years ahead of his time.

His most famous sermon, preached in the West Church,
Boston, on January 30, 1750, was ''A Discourse concerning Unlimited Submission and Non-Resistance to the
Higher Powers.'' Preached on the anniversary of the death
of King Charles the First, Mayhew ''unriddled'' the
doctrine, then preached by the Church of England, that
Charles was ''a saint and a martyr.'' Mayhew took free
rein as he expounded the people's right to resist, even to
execute, such a tyrant.

The sermon was widely read and quoted throughout the
colonies and in Great Britain. It doubtless won for him his
degree of Doctor of Divinity from the University of
Aberdeen in 1751.

We have no knowledge that Jefferson read the sermon,

or that he had its contents in mind when writing the Declaration of Independence. No mention is made of Mayhew in the twenty volumes of Jefferson's collected *Writings*. John Adams may have told Jefferson of Mayhew—indeed, may have presented him with a copy of the famous sermon. But I am willing to concede that the odds are against such a presentation, if not conversation, and to conclude that Jefferson and Mayhew, widely read in many of the same writers on government, arrived at their conclusions independently of each other.

Yet it is interesting to compare parts of Mayhew's sermon with the Declaration of Independence:

"We hold these truths to be self-evident, that all men are created equal, that they are endowed by their Creator with certain unalienable Rights, that among these are Life, Liberty, and the pursuit of Happiness."

Twenty-six years earlier Mayhew said: "Nothing can well be imagined more directly contrary to common sense than to suppose that millions of people should be subjected to the arbitrary, precarious pleasure of a single man,—who has naturally no superiority over them in point of authority,—so that their estates and everything that is valuable in life, and even their lives also, shall be absolutely at his disposal, if he happens to be wanton and capricious enough to demand them."

The Declaration of Independence continues: "That to secure these rights, Governments are instituted among Men, deriving their just powers from the governed."

Twenty-six years earlier Mayhew said: "The only

reason for the institution of civil government, and the only
rational ground for submission to it, is the common safety
and utility.''

The Declaration further states: ''Prudence, indeed will
dictate that Governments long established should not be
changed for light or transient causes; and accordingly all
experience hath shewn, that mankind are more disposed to
suffer, while evils are sufferable, than to right themselves
by abolishing the forms to which they are accustomed.''

Paralleling this observation, Mayhew admitted: ''Now,
as all men are fallible, it cannot be supposed that the public
affairs of any state should be always administered in the
best manner possible, even by persons of the greatest
wisdom and integrity. Nor is it sufficient to legitimate
disobedience to the higher powers that they are not so
administered, or that they are in some instances very
ill-managed; for upon this principle it is scarcely suppos-
able that any government at all could be supported.''

Continuing, Jefferson wrote: ''But when a long train of
abuses and usurpations, pursuing invariably the same
object evinces a design to reduce them under absolute
Despotism, it is their right, it is their duty, to throw off
such a Government, and to provide new Guards for their
future Security.''

Mayhew in 1750 expressed the identical point of view:

''Those in authority may abuse their trust and power to
such a degree that neither the law of reason nor of religion
requires that any obedience or submission be paid to them;
but on the contrary that they should be totally discarded,

The ''Old Brick'' or First Church,
Boston

and the authority which they were before vested with transferred to others, who may exercise more to those good purposes for which it is given.''

The Declaration of Independence then lists the ''repeated injuries and usurpations'' of King George III, among which are these:

''He has refused his assent to laws, the most wholesome and necessary for the public good.

''He has dissolved Representative Houses repeatedly, for opposing with manly firmness his invasions on the rights of the people.

''He has obstructed the Administration of Justice by refusing his Assent to Laws for establishing Judiciary powers (etc.).''

Twenty-six years earlier, Mayhew constructed a similar case against King Charles I: ''During a reign, or rather a tyranny of many years, he governed in a perfectly wild and arbitrary manner, paying no regard to the constitution and the laws of the kingdom, by which the power of the crown was limited . . . He levied many taxes upon the people without the consent of Parliament, and then imprisoned great numbers of the principal merchants and gentry for not paying them. He erected or at least revived several arbitrary courts, in which the most unheard-of barbarities were committed with his knowledge and approbation (etc.).''

I repeat my opinion that Jefferson probably was not acquainted with Mayhew's sermon, ''Concerning Unlimited Submission.'' But I trust that the above parallelism shows not only that "great minds run in the same channel," but also that "Jonathan Mayhew said it first." For a generation before 1776, the congregations of New England had heard and read many "declarations of independence." Sermon after sermon referred to the "natural rights of life, liberty, and property." But to Jonathan Mayhew belongs the distinction of being the first of the Revolutionary preacher-patriots. His sermon of 1750 has long and appropriately been called: "The Morning Gun of the American Revolution."

Mayhew was an intimate of James Otis, John Adams, and Samuel Adams. It was he who suggested to Otis, in a letter dated June 8, 1766, the idea of Committees of Correspondence, which later rendered invaluable service to the patriot cause.

"Would it not be proper and decorous [he wrote Otis] for our assembly to send circulars to all the rest, on the late repeal of the Stamp Act and the present favorable aspect of affairs? . . . Pursuing this course, or never losing sight of it, may be of greatest importance to the colonies, perhaps the only means of perpetuating their liberties."

Six weeks later, on July 19, 1766, Mayhew died of a nervous fever, no doubt the result of overwork.

In the *Massachusetts Gazette* (July 25, 1766), the following lines appear "for the consolation of the late Rev. Dr. Mayhew's Spouse":

"Whilst I attempt in fun'ral Verse
Great MAYHEW'S Virtues to rehearse

Assist me, O Urania! lend your Lays
That I with you may celebrate his praise . . .
Look through his Writings, read his Works sublime,
And they alone declare him all divine.
Virtue was what he practiced, what he taught,
From her he never swerved in deed or thought . . .

Methinks I see him with the Angelic Choir
Chanting the praises of his heav'nly Sire;
Participating of those heav'nly Sweets
Which Christ obtained by his bloody Sweats . . .

So you'll ascend up to the Realms of Love
And join the Chorus with your Spouse above."

Unfortunately, Mayhew did not read the elegy, for if he
had seen it, he would promptly have set the would-be poet
to reading Milton for the improvement of his verse and the
Gospels for the improvement of his theology!

Dr. Charles Chauncy in his *Funeral Discourse* did far
greater justice to the life and work of Jonathan Mayhew:
"Few surpassed him either in the quickness of his apprehension, the clearness of his perception, the readiness
of his invention, the brightness of his imagination, the
comprehension of his understanding, or the soundness of
his judgment . . . He was eminently a friend to liberty both
civil and religious."

Mayhew, like Moses, was granted only a glimpse of the
Promised Land of Liberty. If he had been permitted to live
and to continue his fight for freedom— I shall not indulge
the fancy. Something it is that he should be for a great

contemporary, ''The Father of Civil and Religious Liberty in Massachusetts and America.''

SAMUEL COOPER (1725-1783)

Samuel Cooper was one of the half dozen most influential Bostonians during the American Revolution. He was born in Boston, prepared for college in the Boston Latin School, graduated from Harvard in 1743, and was pastor of the Brattle Street Church for nearly forty years. Boston for him was the hub, spokes, rim, and all.

Cooper served as a member of the Harvard Corporation from 1763 to 1783. He was elected president of Harvard in 1774, but declined the position. It is interesting that his father, the Rev. William Cooper, was also elected to and promptly declined the Harvard presidency. Both father and son considered their life's work to be in the ministry of the Brattle Street Church.

Samuel Cooper was not only a vigorous preacher in behalf of the patriot cause, but also a stirring writer. Daring articles of protest against the Stamp Act and other ''intolerable legislation'' appeared above his signature in the *Boston Gazette*. As a result of his fiery preaching and writing, the British officers made him a favored object of abuse. In 1775 his Church was turned into a barracks for British soldiers.

He was a close friend of Benjamin Franklin, John and Samuel Adams. John Hancock was one of his faithful parishioners. Hancock's ''Fifth of March Oration,'' as well as other papers, has been attributed to Cooper's pen.

The importance of his personal contacts and correspondence is revealed by three successive notations in his *Diary:*

"*July 5, 1775:* Went in my horse and chaise with Mrs. Cooper to Cambridge . . . I waited on General Washington, Lee, Major Miffling, Reed, etc. Dined with General Washington, (and) the other gentlemen . . . Went P.M. to the lines of Prospect Hill. Saw the encampment of British Troops on Bunkers Hill . . .

"*July 6:* Called at the Room of Committee of Safety, and conversed with them. Met at Major Johonnet's Quarters, Col. Bowers and Lady. Called at Congress. Received letters from John and Sam Adams and Mr. Cushing bro't by General Washington . . .

"*July 7:* I wrote Letters to Messrs. Adams, Hancock, Cushing, Dr. Franklin, Madam Hancock." (His *Diary* is reproduced in the *American Historical Review*, VI, 2, 301-341)

In the *Writings* of Samuel Adams may be seen a score of letters written to Cooper between 1775 and 1781. In a letter from Philadelphia dated April 3, 1776, Adams wrote Cooper, "I wish your Leisure would admit of your frequently favoring me with your Thoughts on public affairs." And on December 25, 1778, Adams wrote him: "I hope before long to think aloud with you and my other confidential friends in Boston."

Cooper corresponded even more frequently and intimately with Benjamin Franklin. In 1770, Franklin wrote:

Dr. Samuel Cooper

"You have given, in a little Compass, so full and comprehensive a View of the Circumstances on which is founded the Security Britain has for all reasonable Advantages from us, . . . that I cannot refrain communicating an extract of your Letter, where I think it may be of Use; and I think I shall publish it." Both in 1772 and 1773 Franklin urged Cooper to write him more often—"Your candid, clear, and well written Letters, be assured, are of great use." When Franklin was in France, Cooper kept him in touch with American events and sentiment.

During a glorious ministry of forty years in one church, and an unassuming, patriotic statesmanship from 1763 to 1783, Samuel Cooper lived his abundant life. With restrained words, Tudor writes in his *Life of James Otis:* "Dr. Cooper was a fine scholar . . . He wrote with elegance, and his delivery was eloquent. He had a readiness of thought and flow of language, that gave him great command over his hearers, whether in the pulpit or in conversation. His manners were polished and courteous . . . These qualifications secured to him the private affection and admiration of his parishioners; while his knowledge of the world, and the interest he took in public affairs procured him the esteem and confidence of many public characters."

JONAS CLARK

Jonas Clark of Lexington was one of the most colorful and versatile of the Revolutionary patriot-preachers. Shortly after graduating from Harvard College (1752), he settled in Lexington for a pastorate of exactly fifty years. Like many of his profession, he was a farmer as well as a minister. To support his flock of children he must have found it necessary to augment his meagre annual salary of eighty pounds and twenty cords of wood with the income from his sixty acre farm. (Bowen in his *Lexington Epitaphs* reports that every morning Clark stood at the foot of the staircase and called the family roll: "Polly, Betsey, Lucy, Liddy, Patty, Sally, Thomas, Jonas, William, Peter, Bowen, Harry — Get up! Woe to the delinquent!")

From 1762 until 1776 he drew up a series of town papers, giving instructions to the representatives sent by the town to the general court. He instructed the Lexington delegates to the Stamp Act Congress. Throughout that stormy period, he was the most influential politician as well as churchman in the Lexington-Concord area.

Mr. Clark's home was a rendezvous for many of the patriot leaders. On the very night of April 18, 1775, John Hancock and Samuel Adams were being entertained by Jonas Clark. Paul Revere warned them of the approach of Gage's expedition, one of the objects of which was to capture the Boston patriots. When asked by his guests that night if the Lexington people would fight, Clark is said to have replied: "I have trained them for this very hour."

It was but a few rods from the parsonage that the first blood of the Revolution was shed on the following day, April 19, and the men who fell were his parishioners. Upon seeing the slain, Clark observed: "From this day will be dated the liberty of the world."

Several of his sermons were published, the most
noteworthy being, "The Fate of Blood-thirsty Oppressors," delivered on the first anniversary of the battle of
Lexington. His description of the battle, appended to the
sermon, is a priceless historical document.

In 1799, Jonas Clark was appointed the delegate from
Lexington to the Massachusetts Constitutional Conven-
tion, where he served on several important committees.

OTHER WATCHMEN ON LIBERTY'S WALL

Dr. Charles Chauncy was also considered by John
Adams to be among the half-dozen foremost Revolutionary leaders from Massachusetts. For sixty years, from
1727 to 1787, Chauncy was the minister of the First
Church in Boston. He was regarded as the dean of the
Boston parsons. While he did not enjoy an intimate
friendship with as many leaders as Cooper did, his influence was highly regarded. His sermons, newspaper articles, and pamphlets were more widely distributed in
Europe than those of any propagandist for the American
cause. His Thanksgiving Sermon on the Repeal of the
Stamp Act (1766) bristles with arguments in favor of
resistance against British tyranny.

*   *   *   *   *

While the Rev. Amos Adams does not stand in the front
rank of pulpit statesmen, the memorial tablet in the First
Parish Church, Roxbury, summarizes his work:

Rev. Charles Chauncy

AMOS ADAMS
Scholar, Patriot, Man of God

Led his flock through the stormy days preceding the
   Revolution
Reproved, rebuked, exhorted, with long suffering and
   doctrine
Death came from exposure in preaching to the army
   in front of the church
Born 1728   Ordained 1753   Died 1775

During the Revolution many ministers descended from
the "Wall of Liberty" in order to engage actively in the
fray. Baldwin's *New England Clergy and the American
Revolution* (pp. 154-167) gives an impressive list of their
activities:

"When the news of Lexington and Bunker Hill arrived,
parson after parson left his parish and marched hastily
toward Boston. Before daylight on the morning of April
30, 1775, Stephen Farrar, of New Ipswich, New Hampshire, left with ninety-seven of his parishioners. Joseph
Willard, of Beverly, marched with two companies from his
town, raised in no small part through his own exertion.
David Avery, of Windsor, Vermont, after hearing the
news of Lexington, preached a farewell sermon, then,
outside the meeting-house door, called his people to arms,
and marched with twenty men. On his way he served as
captain, preached, and collected more troops. David
Grosvenor, of Grafton, left his pulpit and, musket in hand,
joined the minute-men who marched to Cambridge.
Phillips Payson, of Chelsea, is given credit for leading a

group of his parishioners to attack a band of English soldiery that nineteenth day of April. Benjamin Balch, of Danvers, Lieutenant of the third-alarm list of his town, was present at Lexington and later, as chaplain in army and navy, won the title of the 'fighting parson.' Jonathan French, of Andover, Massachusetts, left his pulpit on the Sabbath morning, when the news of Bunker Hill arrived, and with surgical case in one hand and musket in the other started for Boston.''

Many who did not join in the actual fighting rendered service to the American cause through preaching and writing, encouraging non-importation of goods and home manufacture, giving of their small salaries to the cause of liberty, and serving as recruiting agents in towns and villages.

CONCLUSION

There is probably no group of men in history, living in a particular area at a given time, who can speak as forcibly on the subject of liberty as the Congregational ministers of New England between 1750 and 1785.

In a day when our liberties are threatened by pressure groups at home and by totalitarian philosophies and wars from abroad, we may well hearken to these ''Watchmen on the Wall.'' Although their wisdom has been ignored by our generation, they can tell us much about the nature of liberty which is relevant for our day. They can tell us from sacrificial experience of the cost of liberty. But, perhaps most important of all, they can help us *root* our passion for liberty deep in the soil of American tradition, as well as Providential creation. Their age taught them, as our age teaches us, that democracy and the religion of Jesus are closely allied; when one falls the other is likely to follow. "Where the spirit of the Lord is, there is liberty"—a favorite text of the Revolutionary ministers—may well be the watchword of freedom in every age.

I

The Divine Source of Liberty

ALL POWER IS FROM GOD

All power is originally from God, and civil government his institution, and is designed to advance the happiness of his creatures. Civil power ought therefore ever to be employed agreeable to the nature and will of the supreme Sovereign and Guardian of all our rights.

Benjamin Stevens, A.M., of Kittery; Mass. Election Sermon, 1761.

HE SAT AT THE HELM

Though our civil joy [for the repeal of the Stamp Act] has been expressed in a decent, orderly way, it would be but a poor, pitiful thing should we rest here, and not make our religious, grateful acknowledgments to the Supreme Ruler of the world, to whose superintending providence it is to be ascribed that we have had 'given us so great deliverance.' Whatever were the means or instruments in order to this, that glorious Being, whose throne is in the heavens and whose kingdom ruleth over all, had the chief hand herein. He sat at the helm, and so governed all things relative to it as to bring it to this happy issue. It was under his all-wise, overruling influence that a spirit was raised up in all the colonies nobly to assert their freedom as men and English-born subjects.

Charles Chauncy, D.D., of the First Church, Boston, Thanksgiving Sermon, 1766.

AGREEABLE TO THE DIVINE WILL

The form of civil government is not of divine appointment; this is left by God very much to the will and determination of men, and depends upon a people's temper, genius, situation, and advantages or disadvantages of various kinds. But yet that form of government which is adopted and established by the consent and agreement of the body of the people, and which is found by experience to be conducive to the common good and interest of society, is that which seems to be agreeable to the divine will.

Ebenezer Bridge, A.M., of Chelmsford; Mass. Election Sermon, 1767.

FOR HIS OWN GLORY

The supreme ruler and governor of the universe hath so adjusted things in the moral world, that order and government are necessary for advancing his own glory, and promoting the good of his rational, intelligent creatures. And it is very obvious that anarchy and confusion must

terminate in the destruction of men's lives, as well as of
their liberty and property.

Ebenezer Bridge, A.M., of Chelmsford; Mass. Election Sermon, 1767.

GOD NEVER GIVES MEN UP

God never gives men up to be slaves till they lose their
national virtue, and abandon themselves to slavery.

Richard Salter, A.M., of Mansfield; Conn. Election Sermon, 1768.

LIFE, LIBERTY, AND PROPERTY

Life, liberty, and property are the gifts of the Creator.

Daniel Shute, A.M., of Hingham; Mass. Election Sermon, 1768.

THE WILL OF HEAVEN AND THE PEOPLE

Government is divinely authorized, and it is the will of
heaven that it should be: but every people (acting freely)
have a right to enjoy their own government.

Eliphalet Williams, M.A., of Hartford; Conn. Election Sermon, 1769.

NEXT TO THE GOSPEL OF PEACE

Next to the gospel of peace, civil government bespeaks
the great good-will of the Most High, to the children of
men.

Eliphalet Williams, M.A., of Hartford; Conn. Election Sermon, 1769.

MINISTERS OF GOD FOR GOOD

Rulers are appointed for this very end—to be ministers
of God for good. The people have a right to expect this
from them, and to require it, not as an act of grace, but as
their reasonable due. It is the express or implicit condition

upon which they were chosen and continued in public office, that they attend continually upon this very thing. Their time, their abilities, their authority—by their acceptance of the public trust—are consecrated to the community, and cannot in justice be withheld. . . . In justice to people, and in faithfulness to God, they must either sustain it with fidelity, or resign the office.

Samuel Cooke, A.M., of Cambridge; Mass. Election Sermon, 1770.

LIBERTY FOR HIS PEOPLE

Christ came to set up a kingdom diverse, indeed, from the kingdoms of this world, but it was no part of his design to put down or destroy government and rule among men. He came to procure liberty for his people, and to make them free in the most important sense, yet not to exempt them from subjection to civil powers, or to dissolve their obligations to one another, as members of political bodies.

John Tucker, A.M., of Newbury; Mass. Election Sermon, 1771.

THE DICTATE OF NATURE

Civil government is not indeed so from God as to be expressly appointed by him in his word. Much less is any particular form of it there delineated as a standing model for the nations of the world. Nor are there any particular persons pointed out as having, in a lineal descent, an indefeasible right to rule over others.

But civil government may be said to be from God, as it is he who qualifies men for, and in his overruling providence, raises them to places of authority and rule . . . Especially and chiefly as civil government is founded in the very nature of man, as a social being, and in the nature and constitution of things. It is manifestly for the good of society. It is the dictate of nature. It is the voice of reason, which may be said to be the voice of God.

John Tucker, A.M., of Newbury; Mass. Election Sermon, 1771.

THE SCRIPTURES AND FREEDOM

The Scriptures cannot be rightfully expounded without explaining them in a manner friendly to the cause of freedom.

Charles Turner, A.M., of Duxbury; Mass. Election Sermon, 1773.

THEY CALL US SAINTS!

If God be for us, who can be against us? The enemy has reproached us for calling on his name, and professing our trust in him. They have made a mock of our solemn fasts, and every appearance of serious Christianity in the land. On this account, by way of contempt, they call us saints; and that they themselves may keep at the greatest distance from this character, their mouths are full of horrid blasphemies, cursing, and bitterness, and vent all the rage of malice and barbarity. And may we not be confident that the Most High, who regards these things, will vindicate his own honor, and plead our righteous cause against such enemies to his government, as well as our liberties. O, may our camp be free from every accursed thing! May our land be purged from all its sins! May we be truly a holy people, and all our towns cities of righteousness.

Samuel Langdon, D.D., President of Harvard College; Mass. Election Sermon, 1775.

NO MURMURING WORD

Neither the insults of oppressors, nor the flames of our once delightful habitations, nor even the innocent blood of our brethren slain, should move us to a murmuring word or an angry thought against God, his government, or providence . . . The more grievously we are smitten, the more deeply we are affected, the more carefully should we endeavor to realize our dependence upon God.

Jonas Clark, A.M., of Lexington; "A Sermon to Commemorate the Murder, Bloodshed, and Commencement of Hostilities," April 19, 1776.

NONE BUT GOD

Unlimited submission and obedience is due to none but God alone. He has an absolute right to command; he alone has an uncontrollable sovereignty over us, because he alone is unchangeably good. He never will nor can require of us, consistent with his nature and attributes, anything which is not fit and reasonable. His commands are all just and good. And to suppose that he has given to any particular set of men a power to require obedience to that which is unreasonable, cruel, and unjust, is robbing the Deity of his justice and goodness.

Samuel West, A.M., of Dartmouth; Mass. Election Sermon, 1776.

PROVIDENCE HAS DESIGNED THIS CONTINENT

For my part, when I consider the dispensations of Providence toward this land ever since our fathers first settled in Plymouth, I find abundant reason to conclude that the great Sovereign of the universe has planted a vine in this American wilderness which he has caused to take deep root, and it has filled the land, and that he will never suffer it to be plucked up or destroyed.

Our fathers fled from the rage of prelatical tyranny and persecution, and came into this land to enjoy liberty of conscience, and they have increased to a great people . . . Could I see a spirit of repentance and reformation prevail through the land, I should not have the slightest apprehension of fear of being brought under the iron rod of slavery, even though all the powers of the globe were combined against us. And though I confess that the irreligion and profaneness which are so common among us give something of a damp to my spirits, yet I cannot help hoping, and even believing, that Providence has designed this continent for to be the asylum of liberty and true religion.

Samuel West, A.M., of Dartmouth; Mass. Election Sermon, 1776.

GOVERNMENT FOR GOOD

But, depend upon it, *no government is God's ordinance but that which is for the good of mankind.*

Samuel Webster, A.M., of Salisbury; Mass. Election Sermon, 1777.

WHEN WE CONSIDER

In the rise and in the whole progress of the unnatural controversy between Great Britain and the now United Independent American States, the hand of God has been, I must think, very conspicuous. When we consider the remarkable union of thirteen disconnected, and many of them distant provinces, and the spirit, which burst forth like a flame nearly at the same time in all parts of the land; when we consider the weak, defenseless, and unprepared state of the country when hostilities were commenced, and in what an unexpected manner, and how quick, a supply of military stores was obtained; when we consider the mighty force that has come against us, both by sea and land, and the success that has attended our young troops and even our militia in many warm encounters with European regular forces; when we consider the little, the very little progress that our enemy has made toward accomplishing their injurious design in three successive campaigns, . . . who can refrain his astonishment, and adoration of the supream [sic] invisible hand that rules the world.

Chauncey Whittelsey, A.M., of New Haven; Conn. Election Sermon, 1778.

PLAIN DICTATES

We want not, indeed, a special revelation from Heaven to teach us that men are born equal and free; that no man has a natural claim of dominion over his neighbors, nor any one nation any such claim upon another; and as government is only the administration of the affairs of a number of men combined for their own security and happiness, such a society have a right freely to determine by whom and in what manner their own affairs shall be administered. These are the plain dictates with which the Common Parent of men has informed the human bosom.

Samuel Cooper, D.D., of Boston; Mass. Election Sermon, 1780.

II

Our Heritage of Liberty

A VIRTUOUS SET OF MEN

God forbid that any son of New England should prove such a profane Esau as to sell his birthright! Our ancestors, though not perfect and infallible in all respects, were a religious, brave, and virtuous set of men, whose love of liberty, civil and religious, brought them from their native land into the American deserts. By their generous care it is, under the smiles of a gracious providence, that we have now here a goodly heritage.

Jonathan Mayhew, D.D., of Boston; Mass. Election Sermon, 1754.

THOSE MASCULINE PRINCIPLES

The rough Saxons imported those masculine principles of Freedom and Government, that equipoise of Power and Liberty which, built upon and improved, have rendered the British Constitution the admiration and envy of the world.

Thomas Barnard, A.M., of Salem; Mass. Election Sermon, 1763.

FOR SAFETY AND DEFENSE

Early did the first settlers of this country discover a due concern, a provident care for themselves and posterity, in making the best provision in their power for safety and defense. No sooner was society formed and civil government established, but, even in their infant state, they made it their care to put the militia of the country upon a respectable footing.

Jonas Clark, A.M., of Lexington; Sermon on "The Importance of Military Skill," 1768.

WHAT WE ENJOY BY CHARTER

What we enjoy by charter is not to be looked upon barely as a matter of *grace;* but, in a measure at least, of *right.* Our fathers faithfully performed the Conditions on which charter privileges were granted.

Jason Haven, A.M., of Dedham; Mass. Election Sermon, 1769.

THE SCENE BRIGHTENS

The season indeed is dark; but God is our sun and shield. When we consider the days of old, and the years of ancient time, the scene brightens, our hopes revive. Our fathers trusted in God; he was their help and their shield.

These ever-memorable worthies, nearly a century and a half since, by the prevalence of spiritual and civil tyranny, were driven from their delightful native land to seek a quiet retreat in these uncultivated ends of the earth; and, however doubtful it might appear to them, or others, whether the lands they were going to possess were properly under the English jurisdiction, yet our ancestors were desirous of retaining a relation to their native country, and to be considered as subjects to the same prince. They left their native land with the strongest assurances that they and their posterity should enjoy the privileges of free, natural-born English subjects, which they supposed fully comprehended in their charter. The powers of government therein confirmed to them they considered as including English liberty in its full extent; and however defective their charter might be in form,—a thing common in that day,—yet the spirit and evident intention of it appears to be then understood.

Samuel Cooke, A.M., of Cambridge; Mass. Election Sermon, 1770.

AS HE WAS WITH OUR FATHERS

But while, in imitation of our pious forefathers, we are aiming at the security of our liberties, we should all be concerned to express by our conduct their piety and virtue, and in a day of darkness and general distress carefully avoid everything offensive to God or injurious to men . . . Let every attempt to secure our liberties be conducted with a manly fortitude, but with that respectful decency which reason approves and which alone gives weight to the most salutary measures. Let nothing divert us from the paths of truth and peace, which are the ways of God, and then we may be sure that he is with us, as he was with our fathers, and never leave nor forsake us.

Samuel Cooke, A.M., of Cambridge; Mass. Election Sermon, 1770.

EXTENSIVE BUSINESS

The God of nature has taught us by the situation and uncommon advantages of this place, that it was designed for extensive business: and here our fathers planted themselves, that they and their posterity might prosecute those branches of trade and merchandise which give riches and strength to nations and states.

John Lathrop, A.M., of Boston; Thanksgiving Sermon, 1774.

CONNECTED BY TIES

Britons and Americans, subjects of the same Crown, connected by the ties of nature, by interest and religion, maintained the most perfect harmony, and felt the purest joy in each other's happiness for more than a hundred years: And would to God, that harmony had never been disturbed.

John Lathrop, A.M., of Boston; Thanksgiving Sermon, 1774.

AS GOOD AS THE PEOPLE OF ENGLAND

As no body on earth had any title to this land but the *original inhabitants*—our fathers got leave of them to settle, and made peace with them, and fairly *purchased* their lands of them.

The king has no right to give it, nor the people of England, for it is not theirs to give. But God gave our fathers favor in the eyes of the people of the land; and they obtained *their title* to these lands; which was as good as the people of England have to theirs, or any other people under heaven. All pretenses to the contrary are vain and frivolous to the last degree.

Samuel Webster, A.M., of Salisbury; Sermon, ''The Misery and Duty of an Enslaved People,'' 1774.

DEEP INWROUGHT AFFECTION

It bears the harder on our spirits when we recollect the deep inwrought affection we have always had for the parent state—our well known loyalty to our Sovereign, and our unremitting attachment to his illustrious house, as well as the ineffable toils, hardships, and dangers which our Fathers endured, unassisted but by heaven, in planting this American wilderness, and turning it into a fruitful field.

Gad Hitchcock, A.M., of Pembroke; Mass. Election Sermon, 1774.

A MERE SHADOW

The excellency of the constitution has been the boast of Great Britain and the envy of the neighboring nations. In former times the great departments of the state, and the various places of trust and authority were filled by men of wisdom, honesty, and religion, who employed all their powers, and were ready to risk their fortunes and their lives for the common good. They were faithful counsellors to king; directed their authority and majesty to the happiness of the nation, and opposed every step by which despotism endeavored to advance. They were fathers of the people, and sought the welfare and prosperity of the whole body

. . . Religion discovered its general influence among all ranks, and kept out great corruptions from places of power.

But in what does the British nation now glory? In a mere shadow of its ancient political system; in titles of dignity without virtue; in vast public treasures continually lavished in corruption till every fund is exhausted, notwithstanding the mighty streams perpetually flowing in; in the many artifices to stretch the prerogatives of the crown beyond all constitutional bounds, and to make the king an absolute monarch, while the people are deluded with a mere phantom of liberty.

Samuel Langdon, D.D., President of Harvard College; Mass. Election Sermon, 1775.

BORN FREE

No man denies but that *originally* all were equally free. Men did not purchase their freedom, nor was it the grant of kings, nor from charter, covenant, or compact, nor in any proper sense from man: But from God. They were born free.

But, behold, sin reign'd and disturb'd the peace of men. And then tyrants presently began to reign also. Like our clothing they are the mark of lost innocence. The people trusting too much power in the hands of some to defend them, they presently used it to oppress them. . . .

Gross ignorance and sloth in the people must lay the foundation. Ignorance is as much the mother of slavery as popish devotion.

Samuel Webster, A.M., of Salisbury; Mass. Election Sermon, 1777.

FROM THE LOVE OF LIBERTY

We stand this day upon Pisgah's top, the children of the free woman, the descendants of a pious race, who from the love of liberty and the fear of God, spent their treasure and spilt their blood. Animated by the same great spirit of liberty, and determined under God to be free, these states have made one of the noblest stands against despotism and tyranny that can be met with in the annals of history, either ancient or modern. One common cause, one common danger, and one common interest has united and urged us to the most vigorous executions. From small beginnings, from great weakness, impelled from necessity and the tyrant's rod, but following the guidance of heaven, we have gone through a course of noble and heroic actions, with minds superior to the most virulent menaces, and to all the horrors of war, for we trusted in the God of our forefathers.

Phillips Payson, A.M., of Chelsea; Mass. Election Sermon, 1778.

III

The Nature of Liberty

IT IS THEIR FELICITY

It is their felicity [as British Subjects] to be governed by such men and by such laws as themselves approve; without which their boasted liberty would, indeed, be but an empty name.

Jonathan Mayhew, D.D., of Boston; Mass. Election Sermon, 1754.

THOSE SALUTARY PURPOSES

Civil government is absolutely necessary to public happiness. But without good laws and wholesome institutions, government cannot subsist. At least it can never answer those salutary purposes for which it was appointed.

Noah Welles, A.M., of Stamford; Conn. Election Sermon, 1764.

WHERE PUBLIC SPIRIT PREVAILS

Liberty is the glory of a community, the most firm and

unshaken basis of public happiness. The want of this will abate the value of all the comforts of life. The embittering circumstance of precarious property,—the grating reflection that life and all its enjoyments lie at the mercy of a tyrant, and are liable every moment to be ravished by the lawless hand of violence,—mars the relish of every gratification, and throws a melancholy gloom upon all temporal enjoyments. But wherever public spirit prevails, liberty is secure. There men may think freely for themselves, and publish their sentiments without molestation or fear. For as liberty is the source of so much public-happiness, he who is a patriot, and wishes well to his country, must needs be a fast friend to it.

Noah Welles, A.M., of Stamford; Conn. Election Sermon, 1764.

WITHOUT EXTRAORDINARY PENETRATION

People are generally capable of knowing when they are well used. Public happiness is easily felt. Men cannot but perceive when they enjoy their rights and privileges; when the laws of the land have their course, and justice is impartially administered; when no unreasonable burdens are laid upon them; when their rulers are ready to hear their complaints and to redress their wrongs . . . Such a temper and conduct in rulers are easily perceived without any extraordinary penetration.

Andrew Eliot, A.M., of Boston; Mass. Election Sermon, 1765.

THE COLONISTS ARE MEN

The colonists are men, and need not be afraid to assert

the natural rights of men; they are British subjects, and may justly claim the common rights, and all the privileges of such, with plainness and freedom. And from what lately occurred, there is reason to hope the Parliament will ever hereafter be willing to hear and grant our just requests; especially if any grievances should take place so great, so general, and alarming, as to unite all the colonies in petitioning for redress, as with one voice.

Jonathan Mayhew, D.D., of Boston; Sermon, "The Snare Broken," 1766.

THE BALANCE OF POWER

Happy are those whose political plan allows such prerogative as is sufficient to the vigor, uniformity, and dispatch of public measures, but at the same time with such restrictions, that the liberties of the subject are safe . . . The balance of power in a mixed government is no empty theory. The destruction of it is terrible.

Edward Barnard, A.M., of Haverhill; Mass. Election Sermon, 1776.

A GOOD CONSTITUTION

A good constitution of government, such as one that secures the mutual dependence of the sovereign or ruling powers, and the people on each other, and which secures the rights of each, and the good of the whole society, is a great blessing to a people.

Ebenezer Bridge, A.M., of Chelmsford; Mass. Election Sermon, 1767.

HENCE ARISES GOVERNMENT

Although there is a natural inequality and independency

among men, yet they have voluntarily combined together, and by compact and mutual agreement, have entered into a social state, and bound themselves to the performance of a multitude of affairs, tending to the good; and to the avoiding of a multitude of injuries tending to the hurt and damage of the whole. And hence arises order and government, and a just regulation of all those matters which relate to the safety of the persons, lives, liberties, and property of individuals.

Ebenezer Bridge, A.M., of Chelmsford; Mass. Election Sermon, 1767.

THE CIVIL CONSTITUTION

A compact for civil government in any community implies the stipulation of certain rules of government. These rules or laws more properly make the civil constitution. How various these rules are in different nations is not the present enquiry; but that they ought in every nation to coincide with the moral fitness of things, by which alone the natural rights of mankind can be secured, and their happiness promoted, is very certain. And such are the laws of the constitution of civil government that we, and all British subjects are so happy to live under.

Daniel Shute, A.M., of Hingham; Mass. Election Sermon, 1768.

A RICH COMPENSATION

By forming into civil society, men do indeed give up much of their natural rights; but it is in prospect of a rich compensation, in the better security of the rest, and in the enjoyment of several additional ones, that flow from the constitution of government which they establish.

Jason Haven, A.M., of Dedham; Mass. Election Sermon, 1769.

THE LAW AND THE MAN

The best constitution, separately considered, is only as a line that marks out the inclosure, or as a fitly organized body without spirit or animal life. The advantages of civil government, even under the British form, greatly depend upon the character and conduct of those to whom the administration is committed. When the righteous are in authority, the people rejoice; but when the wicked beareth rule, the people mourn.

Samuel Cooke, A.M., of Cambridge; Mass. Election Sermon, 1770.

NOT TO ENNOBLE A FEW

The people, the collective body only, have a right, under God, to determine who shall exercise the trust for the common interest, and to fix the bounds of their authority; and, consequently, unless we admit the most evident inconsistence, those in authority, in the whole of their public conduct, are accountable to the society which gave them their political existence. This is evidently the natural origin and state of all civil government, the sole end and design of which is, not to ennoble a few and enslave the multitude, but the public benefit, the good of the people; that they may be protected in their persons, and secured in the enjoyment of all their rights, and be enabled to lead quiet and peaceable lives in all godliness and honesty.

While this manifest design of civil government, under whatever form, is kept in full view, the reciprocal obligations of rulers and subjects are obvious, and the extent of prerogative and liberty will be indisputable.

Samuel Cooke, A.M., of Cambridge; Mass. Election Sermon, 1770.

LIKE A BODY IN FULL HEALTH

The springs of government, acting with vigor, and under a right direction, and the members of society yielding a correspondent and uniform submission, a general harmony and happiness must ensue. The political state would be like a body in full health. The constitutional laws, preserved inviolate, would, like strong bones and sinews, support and steady the regular frame. Supreme and subordinate Rulers duly performing their proper functions, would be like the greater and lesser arteries keeping up their proper tone; and justice, fidelity, and every social virtue would, like the vital fluid, run without obstruction, and reach, refresh, and invigorate the most minute and distant parts. While the multitude of subjects yielding, in their various places and relations, a ready and cheerful obedience, would, like the numerous yet connected veins, convey back again the recurrent blood to the great fountain of it, and the whole frame be vigorous, easy, and happy.

John Tucker, A.M., of Newbury; Mass. Election Sermon, 1771.

THE LAWS AND THE MAGISTRATES

It was a fine expression of the Spartan Ruler, and indicated the freedom and happiness of the state, who, upon being asked, "who governed Sparta?" answered, "the laws, and the magistrates according to these laws."

John Tucker, A.M., of Newbury; Mass. Election Sermon, 1771.

NOT ONLY THE CEMENT

The great and wise Author of our being has so formed us that the love of liberty is natural. This passion, like all other original principles of the human mind is, in itself, perfectly innocent and designed for excellent purposes, though like them, liable through abuse of becoming the cause of mischief to ourselves and others. In a civil state, the genius of whose constitution is agreeable to it, this passion, while in its full vigor and under proper regulation, is not only the cement of the political body, but the wakeful guardian of its interests, and the great animating spring of useful and salutary operations; and then only is it injurious to the public or to individuals, when, through misapprehension of things or by being overbalanced by self-love, it takes a wrong direction.

John Tucker, A.M., of Newbury; Mass. Election Sermon, 1771.

ALL MEN ARE IN A STATE OF FREEDOM

All men are naturally in a state of freedom, and have an equal claim to liberty. No one by nature, nor by any special grant from the great Lord of all, has any authority over another. All right, therefore, in any to rule over others, must originate from those they rule over, and be granted by them.

John Tucker, A.M., of Newbury; Mass. Election Sermon, 1771.

LIMITS ARE MARKED OUT

Submission is due to all constitutional laws, whether
they suit the present interest of individuals or not . . .
Unlimited submission, however, is not due to government
in a free state. There are certain boundaries beyond which
submission cannot be justly required, nor is therefore due.
These limits are marked out, and fixt, by the known,
established, and fundamental laws of the state. These laws
being consented to by the governing power, confine as
well as direct its operation and influence, and are the
connecting band between authority and obedience.

John Tucker, A.M., of Newbury; Mass. Election Sermon, 1771.

CAPACITY AND PUBLIC SPIRIT

To answer the purpose of Government, it is of consequence that men should be blessed with capacity, and
possessed of enlarged knowledge, respecting the nature of
their office, the extent of their power, the state of their
sufferings, and dangers of the people, their interests, and
what may conduce to their relief, security, and happiness.
But men of such greatness (like elephants in war) are not to
be *depended* on, as persons who will *steadily* pursue the
publick good, unless they are possessed of that publick
spirit, which the charitable Gospel infuses . . . Publick
spirit carries the magistrate with firmness, uniformity, and
perseverance through his course of duty, however en-
vironed with warping temptations. It inspires him with
compassion, forbids the appearance of oppression. It

quickens to vigilance and activity, renders him a father to the community, a minister of God for good.

Charles Turner, A.M., of Duxbury; Mass. Election Sermon, 1773.

CORRELATES

Rulers and subjects are correlates in free elective states (like this colony); they have a necessary relation to and mutual dependence on each other: Nor can it be otherwise in all respects so long as that relation exists.

Samuel Lockwood, A.M., of Andover; Conn. Election Sermon, 1774.

THE THREE BRANCHES

There is (probably) no human form of government on earth free of all possible inconveniences. And perhaps no one form can suit the state and genius of every nation (if of any one) at all times . . .

But the British legislature, consisting of three branches; *to check, moderate, and temper each other;* it is imagined is preferable to any other we have the knowledge of. God grant the British constitution may long continue.

Samuel Lockwood, A.M., of Andover; Conn. Election Sermon, 1774.

THEIR MEASURES MILD

Religious rulers are, in every view, blessings to society: their laws are just and good, their measures mild and humane, and their example morally engaging.

Gad Hitchcock, A.M., of Pembroke; Mass. Election Sermon, 1774.

A STATE OF NATURE

A state of nature, though it be a state of perfect freedom, yet is far from a state of licentiousness. The law of nature gives men no right to do anything that is immoral, or contrary to the will of God, and injurious to their fellow-creatures; for a state of nature is properly a state of law and government, even a government founded upon the unchangeable nature of the Deity, and a law resulting from the eternal fitness of things. Sooner shall heaven and earth pass away, and the whole frame of nature be dissolved, than any part, even the smallest iota, of this law shall ever be abrogated; it is unchangeable as the Deity himself, being a transcript of his moral perfections . . . Had this subject been properly attended to and understood, the world had remained free from a multitude of absurd and pernicious principles, which have been industriously propagated by artful and designing men, both in politics and divinity. The doctrine of non-resistance and unlimited passive obedience to the worst of tyrants could never have found credit among mankind had the voice of reason been hearkened to for a guide, because such a doctrine would immediately have been discerned to be contrary to natural law.

Samuel West, A.M., of Dartmouth; Mass. Election Sermon, 1776.

THE FIRST FOUNDATION

Where the magistrates and people are generally virtuous, the people may be tolerably happy under almost any constitution, or indeed without any. Yet as the world is, a *good constitution* is by no means to be disregarded; but is the first foundation to be laid for the happiness of the people; and of great importance.

Samuel Webster, A.M., of Salisbury; Mass. Election Sermon, 1777.

FACTIONS IN FREE GOVERNMENT

Free republican governments have been objected to, as if exposed to factions from an excess of liberty. The Grecian states are mentioned for a proof, and it is allowed that the history of some of these commonwealths is little else but a narration of factions. But it is justly denied that the true spirit of liberty produced these effects.

Violent and opposing parties shaking the pillars of state, may arise under the best forms of government. A government from various causes may be thrown into convulsions, like the Roman state in its latter periods, and like that, may die of the malady. But the evils which happen in a state are not always to be charged upon its government, much less upon one of the noblest principles that can dwell in the human breast.

Phillips Payson, A.M., of Chelsea; Mass. Election Sermon, 1778.

RULERS ARE TRUSTEES

Power being a delegation, and all delegated power being in its nature subordinate and limited, hence rulers are but trustees, and government a trust; therefore fidelity is a prime qualification in a ruler; this joined with good natural and acquired abilities, goes far to complete the character.

Phillips Payson, A.M., of Chelsea; Mass. Election Sermon, 1778.

TO PICK THE POCKETS OF A BLIND MAN

The baneful effects of exorbitant wealth, the lust of power, and other evil passions, are so inimical to a free, righteous government, and find such an easy access to the human mind, that it is difficult, if possible, to keep up the spirit of good government, unless the spirit of liberty prevails in the state. This spirit, like other generous growths of nature, flourishes best in its native soil. It has been engrafted at one time or another in various countries: in America it shoots up and grows as in its natural soil . . . It may hence well be expected that the exertions and effects of American liberty should be more vigorous and complete. It has the most to fear from ignorance and avarice; for it is no uncommon thing for a people to lose sight of their liberty in the eager pursuit of wealth, as the states of Holland have done; and it will always be as easy to rob an ignorant people of their liberty as to pick the pockets of a blind man.

Phillips Payson, A.M., of Chelsea; Mass. Election Sermon, 1778.

THE BLESSINGS OF INDEPENDENCE

Independence gives us a rank among the nations of the earth, which no precept of our religion forbids us to understand and feel, and which we should be ambitious to support in the most reputable manner. It opens to us a free communication with all the world, not only for the improvement of commerce, and the acquisition of wealth, but also for the cultivation of the most useful knowledge. It naturally unfetters and expands the human mind, and prepares it for the impression of the most exalted virtues, as well as the reception of the most important science.

Samuel Cooper, D.D., of Boston; Mass. Election Sermon, 1780.

LAWS ON PAPER AND INK

If laws, when made, exist only on paper and ink, what benefit can a people derive from them? The divine law is quick and powerful, and sharper than any two-edged sword; and surely his ministers ought to make the laws, which they execute, bear some resemblance to his.

Moses Mather, M.A., of Middlesex; Conn. Election Sermon, 1781.

IV

The Nature of Tyranny

BY SEASONABLE PRECAUTION

Those nations which are now groaning under the iron scepter of tyranny were once free; so they might probably have remained, by a seasonable precaution against despotic measures. Civil tyranny is usually small in its beginning, like "the drop of a bucket," till at length like a mighty torrent or the raging waves of the sea, it bears down all before it, and deluges whole countries and empires. Thus it is as to ecclesiastical tyranny also—the most cruel, intolerable, and impious of any. From small beginnings "it exalts itself above all that is called God and that is worshipped." People have no security against being unmercifully priest-ridden, but by keeping all imperious bishops and other clergymen who love to "lord it over God's heritage," from getting their foot into the stirrup at all. Let them once be fairly mounted, and their "beasts, the laity'' may prance and flounce about to no purpose; and they will at length be so jaded and hacked by these reverend jockeys, that they will not even have spirits enough to complain that their backs are galled, or, like Balaam's ass, to "rebuke the madness of the prophet."

Jonathan Mayhew, D.D., of Boston; from the Preface to his sermon, "Unlimited Submission and Nonresistance to the Higher Powers," 1750.

THE FOREHEAD TO VENTILATE

It is very strange we should be told at this time of day that loyalty and slavery mean the same thing; though this is plainly the amount of that doctrine which some, even now, have the forehead to ventilate, in order to bring a reproach upon the Revolution (of 1688), upon the present happy settlement of the crown, and to prepare us for the dutiful reception of an *hereditary Tyrant.*

Jonathan Mayhew, D.D., of Boston; from the Preface to his sermon, "Unlimited Submission and Nonresistance to the Higher Powers," 1750.

THE MASK OF PATRIOTISM

'Tis not every pretended regard for our country, or zeal for the public welfare, that deserves the name of public-spirit. There are hypocrites and impostors, wild enthusiasts and frantic zealots in patriotism and politics, as well as in religion. Too often the restless spirit of disaffection and discontent,—the wild zeal of ambition and faction, or the ungovernable fury of sedition, treason, and rebellion, assume the mask of patriotism, artfully mimic the air of public spirit, and endeavor to obtrude themselves upon the world for a disinterested regard for the common happiness. But 'tis not hard for the discerning eye to detect the imposture, and unmask the cheat.

Noah Welles, A.M., of Stamford; Conn. Election Sermon, 1764.

'TIS A MELANCHOLY TRUTH

'Tis a melancholy truth, confirmed by the history of all nations, that the rulers of this world have generally set themselves in opposition to the interest of true religion and the cause of Christ. . . . This was the case for the first three hundred years after the publication of the Christian scheme . . . And even to this day the religion of the gospel labors under much oppression from the greater part of civil rulers.

Edward Dorr, A.M., of Hartford; Conn. Election Sermon, 1765.

MISERABLE TYRANNY

No *tyranny* can be more miserable than *anarchy*.

Eliphalet Williams, M.A., of Hartford; Conn. Election Sermon, 1769.

PRETENSES TO INFALLIBILITY

Arrogant pretenses to infallibility in matters of state or religion, represent human nature in the most contemptible light.

Samuel Cooke, A.M., of Cambridge; Mass. Election Sermon, 1770.

POLITICAL ZEALOTS

There are ambitious and designing men in the state, as well as in the church; and there are fit tools to serve the purposes of both. As some make hereticks in the church, and raise an ecclesiastic posse to demolish them, chiefly with a view to render themselves distinguished, as sound in the faith; so others make traitors in the state, and raise the popular cry against them, to gain to themselves the name of Patriots.

The wise and prudent will make a pause, before they enlist under such political zealots. They will judge for themselves of the faulted conduct of their rulers. They will make reasonable allowances for human frailties, and be as ready to yield submission where it is due, as to defend their liberties when they are in danger.

John Tucker, A.M., of Newbury; Mass. Election Sermon, 1771.

THEY WHO DESERVE THE YOKE

There have been Rulers, and may be such again, who look with wishful eyes on the liberties and privileges of the people. Who consider them as a prey, worthy to be seized, for the gratification of their pride and ambition. . . .

A people in love with liberty and sensible to their rights to it, cannot but be jealous of such Rulers; and ought to be on their guard against unjustifiable and arbitrary claims. Tamely to submit would be highly unworthy of them as free men, and show they deserved the yoke, under which they so readily put their necks.

John Tucker, A.M., of Newbury; Mass. Election Sermon, 1771.

MYSTERIES OF INIQUITY

To have incomprehensible mysteries in Government is the Divine prerogative. Profound secrets in human governments, inaccessible to society, are too liable to become insufferable *mysteries of iniquity.*

Charles Turner, A.M., of Duxbury; Mass. Election Sermon, 1773.

POPERY

That servants of the publick should not be responsible to the publick, is popery, either in religion or politicks.

Charles Turner, A.M., of Duxbury; Mass. Election Sermon, 1773.

UNLIMITED POWER AND THE PEOPLE

Unlimited power has generally been destructive of human happiness. The people are not under such temptations to thwart their own interests, as absolute government is under to abuse the people.

Charles Turner, A.M., of Duxbury; Mass. Election Sermon, 1773.

MOST GRIEVOUS EDICTS

The British administration by the force of great abilities, perverted to base purposes, and by their command of the national treasure, have influenced the Parliament to enact the most grievous edicts against us. Laws made, with the feigned pretense of protecting and securing us, and for the support of civil government, have been the most direct invasion of our property, and subversive of every idea of English freedom.

Joseph Lyman, A.M., of Hatfield; Mass. Election Sermon, 1775.

THE AMAZING NATIONAL DEBT

The pretense for taxing America has been that the nation

contracted an immense debt for the defense of the American colonies, and that as they are now able to contribute some proportion toward the discharge of this debt, and must be considered as part of the nation, it is reasonable they should be taxed . . . But can the amazing national debt be paid by a little trifling sum squeezed from year to year out of America? Would it not be much superior wisdom and sounder policy for a distressed kingdom to retrench the vast unnecessary expenses continually incurred by its enormous vices; to stop the prodigious sums paid in pensions, and to numberless officers, without the least advantage to the public; to reduce the number of devouring servants in the great family; to turn their minds from the pursuit of pleasure and the boundless luxuries of life to the important interests of their country and the salvation of the commonwealth? . . . Millions might annually be saved if the kingdom were generally and thoroughly reformed. But the demands of corruption are constantly increasing, and will forever exceed all the resources of wealth which the wit of man can invent or tyranny impose.

Samuel Langdon, D.D., President of Harvard College; Mass. Election Sermon, 1775.

GRADUAL ENCROACHMENTS ON LIBERTY

Power, especially over-grown power, whets the ambition and sets all the wits to work to enlarge it. Therefore, encroachments on the people's liberties are not generally made all at once, but so gradually as hardly to be perceived by the less watchful; and all plaistered over, it may be, with such plausible pretenses, that before they are aware of the snare, they are taken and cannot disentangle themselves.

Samuel Webster, A.M., of Salisbury; Mass. Election Sermon, 1777.

FOR SHEPHERDS TO BUTCHER

If we look over the prophets [of the Old Testament], we shall find that the rulers are peculiarly guilty: the princes were become mighty oppressors: and when foreign enemies attacked them, unnaturally joined and conspired their ruin! This was a crime of the highest nature. For nothing can be more aggravated than for the *shepherds* to *mislead* and *butcher* the flock they were set to *defend* and *feed!* And the *guardians* of the public interests, to turn *traitors* and *assassins* to them that raised them to their high places!

Samuel Webster, A.M., of Salisbury; Mass. Election Sermon, 1777.

SUCH A PITCH OF ARROGANCE

The business of all in power is to defend the lives, liberties, and property of the people: and they have no other business. Yet every one of these have the great tyrants of the world invaded! They have not only robbed and spoiled them of their property by their violent exactions and by engaging them in needless wars, but at length rose to such a pitch of arrogance as to claim the people and all they had as their property, to be disposed of at their pleasure, as if all the people were made for them and not they for the people!

Samuel Webster, A.M., of Salisbury; Mass. Election Sermon, 1777.

BY OUR VICES

The low and declining state of religion and virtue among us is too obvious not to be seen, and of too threatening an aspect not to be lamented by all the lovers of God and their country. Though our happiness as a community depends much on the conduct of our rulers, yet it is not in the power of the best government to make an impious, profligate people happy. How well soever our public affairs may be managed, we may undo ourselves by our vices. And it is from hence, I apprehend, that our greatest danger arises. That spirit of infidelity, selfishness, luxury, and dissipation, which so deeply marks our present manners, is more formidable than all the arms of our enemies.

Simeon Howard, A.M., of Boston; Mass. Election Sermon, 1780.

V

The Results of Tyranny

THIS HATEFUL MONSTER

Tyranny brings ignorance and brutality along with it. It degrades men from their just rank into the class of brutes; it damps their spirits; it suppresses arts; it extinguishes every spark of noble ardor and generosity in the breasts of those who are enslaved by it; it makes naturally strong and great minds feeble and little, and triumphs over the ruins of virtue and humanity. This is true of tyranny in every shape: there can be nothing great and good where its influence reaches. For which reason it becomes every friend to truth and human kind, every lover of God and the Christian religion, to bear a part in opposing this hateful monster.

Jonathan Mayhew, D.D., of Boston; Preface to sermon, "Unlimited Submission and Nonresistance to the Higher Powers," 1750.

SEEDS IN A PROLIFIC SOIL

To pour contempt upon rulers is to weaken government itself, and to weaken government is to sow the seeds of libertinism, which in a soil so prolific as human nature, will soon spring up into a luxuriant growth.

Daniel Shute, A.M., of Hingham; Mass. Election Sermon, 1768.

ARBITRARY MEASURES

Arbitrary and oppressive measures in the state would indeed dispirit the people and weaken the nerves of industry, and in their consequences lead to poverty and ruins; but a mild and equitable administration will encourage their hearts and strengthen their hands to execute with vigor those measures which promote the strength and safety of the whole.

Daniel Shute, A.M., of Hingham; Mass. Election Sermon, 1768.

PRETENDED MYSTERIES

Mysteries in civil government relative to the rights of the people, like mysteries in the laws of religion, may be pretended,—and to the like purpose of slavery.

Daniel Shute, A.M., of Hingham; Mass. Election Sermon, 1768.

CLEAR GONE!

When right is perverted, justice bought and sold, and bribery, venality, and corruption are countenanced or winked at, and wickedness permitted to triumph and rage without control; the sword lying still or rusting in the scabbard; (then) the public safety and happiness is not only hazarded, but clear gone.

Eliphalet Williams, M.A., of Hartford; Conn. Election Sermon, 1769.

BITTER, BLOODY WATERS

The complaints heard among us are, not only that the Rivers are shifted into other channels, but that the waters are become bitter—yea—that the waters are become bloody.

Moses Parsons, A.M., of Newbury Falls; Mass. Election Sermon, 1772.

THE NOD OF THE TYRANT

The consequences of an arbitrary tyrannic government are most distressing. When the will of the Prince is the law of the subject; when life, liberty, and property lie at the mercy of a Despot; and the nod of the tyrant brings on an execution by the bow and the string—such an administration of government is like an inundation or landflood, which carries all before it.

Moses Parsons, A.M., of Newbury Falls; Mass. Election Sermon, 1772.

OBSTA PRINCIPIIS

The most grasping and oppressive power will commonly let its neighbors remain in peace, if they will submit to its unjust demands. And an incautious people may submit to these demands, one after another, till its liberty is irrecoverably gone . . . We should ever act upon that ancient maxim of prudence: *obsta principiis*.

Simeon Howard, A.M., of Boston; Artillery Election Sermon, 1773.

JEALOUS BRITAIN

If Great Britain is jealous of the increasing interest of the colonies, no doubt she will exert her power to check their growth, or her policy to draw off their riches as fast as they acquire them. And from the measures that have been pursued, with unremitting zeal for several years past, the Americans are made to believe that Great Britain does not wish the colonies to make further advances towards *powerful states.*—The business then is to embarrass new settlements,—to lay such burdens on the colonies now planted as to prevent emigrations to them from the crowded parts of Europe, and establish such laws as shall render, not only the money, but the *persons* of Americans, the property of the British Parliament, or of the crown.

John Lathrop, A.M., of Boston; Thanksgiving Sermon, 1774.

NEEDLESS TAXES

Needless taxes are not for the good, but the misery of the subjects, tending to reduce them to poverty and distress; and may therefore be justly considered as wanton un-disguised oppression, to support the pride, ambition, and extravagance of a few grandees.

Robert Ross, A.M., Stratford; Sermon, "The Union of the Colonies," 1775.

ORDER HAS BEEN PRESERVED

It is now ten months since this colony has been deprived of the benefit of that government which was so long enjoyed by charter. They have had no general assembly for matters of legislation and the public revenue. The courts of justice have been shut up, and almost the whole executive power has ceased to act. Yet order among the people has been remarkably preserved; few crimes have been committed punishable by the judge; even former contentions betwixt one neighbor and another have ceased; nor have fraud and rapine taken advantage of the imbecility of the civil powers.

Samuel Langdon, D.D., of Harvard College; Mass. Election Sermon, 1775.

OUR LATE, HAPPY GOVERNMENT

Our late happy government is changed into the terrors of military execution. Our firm opposition to the establishment of an arbitrary system is called rebellion, and we are to expect no mercy but to yield property and life at discretion. This we are resolved at all events not to do, and therefore we have taken up arms in our own defense, and all the colonies are united in the great cause of liberty.

But how shall we live while civil government is dissolved? What shall we do without counsellors and judges? A state of absolute anarchy is dreadful. Submission to the tyranny of hundreds of imperious masters, firmly embodied against us, and united in the same cruel design of disposing of our lives and subsistence at their pleasure, and making their own will our law in all cases whatsoever, is the vilest slavery, and worse than death.

Samuel Langdon, D.D.; Mass. Election Sermon, 1775.

THE PAPAL YOKE

Christendom would never have been roused from that

state of ignorance, and darkness, and slavery it was in—the *protestant league* would never have been entered into with such firmness and resolution, to shake off the *papal yoke,* and redeem both *church* and *state* from the *hierarchy* of Rome, by which they had been so long oppressed, rose to an intolerable height, and put them upon the expedient.

Jonas Clark, A.M., of Lexington; Sermon, April 19, 1776.

WHERE TYRANNY BEGINS

Where tyranny begins government ends.

Samuel West, of Dartmouth; Mass. Election Sermon at Boston, 1776.

ON THE ESTABLISHMENT OF RELIGION

For the civil authority to pretend to establish particular modes of faith and forms of worship, and to punish all that deviate from the standards which our superiors have set up, is attended with the most pernicious consequences to society. It cramps all free and rational inquiry, fills the world with hypocrites and superstitious bigots—nay, with infidels and skeptics; it exposes men of religion and conscience to the rage and malice of fiery, blind zealots, and dissolves every tender tie of human nature. And I cannot but look upon it as a peculiar blessing of Heaven that we live in a land where everyone can freely deliver his sentiments upon religious subjects, and have the privilege of worshiping God according to the dictates of his own conscience, without any molestation or disturbance—a

privilege which I hope we shall ever keep up and stren-
uously maintain.

Samuel West, A.M., of Dartmouth; Mass. Election Sermon, 1776.

FROM JULIUS TO GEORGE!

Take a brief view of the oppressions of the rulers of the
world. To pretend to give a particular history of this,
would be almost the same thing as to give the history of the
world from Cain to Nimrod, and from him to
Nebuchadnezzar, and from him to Alexander, and from
him to Julius Caesar, and from Julius to George! . . . The
great oppressors of the earth were entrusted with power by
the people to defend them from the little oppressors. The
sword of justice was put into their hands, but behold they
soon turned it into a sword of oppression; and made their
little finger thicker than all their loins of whom the people
were afraid.

And so, in a multitude of instances, the *remedy* has
proved unspeakably worse than the *disease*.

Samuel Webster, A.M., of Salisbury; Mass. Election Sermon, 1777.

DANGEROUS POLITICAL PHYSIC

Coercives in government should always be held as very
dangerous political physic: such as have gone into the
practice have commonly either killed or lost their patients.

Phillips Payson, A.M., of Chelsea; Mass. Election Sermon, 1778.

SHOULD OUR ENEMIES PREVAIL

Should our enemies finally prevail and establish that

absolute dominion over us at which they aim, they would not only render us the most miserable of all nations, but probably be able, by the riches and forces of America, to triumph over the arms of France and Spain, and carry their conquests to every corner of the globe. The noble spirit of Liberty which has arisen in Ireland would be instantly crushed . . . And in every country where this event should be known the friends of liberty would be disheartened, and seeing her in the power of her enemies, forsake her, as the disciples of Christ did their Master; so that our being subdued to the will of our enemies might, in its consequences, be the banishment of liberty from among mankind.

Simeon Howard, A.M., of Boston; Mass. Election Sermon, 1780.

PACIFIC COMMONWEALTHS

Monarchies are often in war, with a view to extend the domains of a single man, while commonwealths are naturally pacific; because the benefit resulting from conquest, being divided among the ruling body, which is numerous and often shifted, or among the community at large, is not a sufficient *stimulus* to war.

Zabdiel Adams, A.M., of Lunenburgh; Sermon preached at Lexington on April 19, 1783.

VI

The Cost of Liberty

FREE AND LOYAL

L et us learn to be free and to be loyal; let us not profess ourselves vassals to the lawless pleasure of any man on earth; but let us remember, at the same time, government is sacred and not to be trifled with. . . . Let us prize our freedom but not "use our liberty for a cloak of maliciousness." There are men who strike at liberty under the term licentiousness; there are others who aim at popularity under the disguise of patriotism. Be aware of both. Extremes are dangerous. There is at present among us, perhaps, more danger of the latter than of the former; for which reason I would exhort you to pay all due regard to the government over us, to the king and all in authority, and to "lead a quiet and peaceable life."

Jonathan Mayhew, D.D., of Boston; Sermon, "Concerning Unlimited Submission," 1750.

NOT BY CLAMORS

It is not by clamors for liberty, or opposition to legal authority, that our invaluable privileges are to be secured; but by seeking and cultivating the spirit of Christ, his holy religion, and a sacred regard to all its requirements and wise institutions.

Benjamin Stevens, A.M., of Kittery; Mass. Election Sermon, 1761.

THE TRUE PATRIOT

The true patriot is one whose purse, as well as his heart, is open for the defense and support of his country.

Noah Welles, A.M., of Stamford; Conn. General Assembly Sermon, 1764.

TO TEMPT ALL HAZARDS

The general discontent [over the Stamp Act] operated very differently upon the minds of different people . . . Some at once grew melancholy, sitting down in a kind of lethargic, dull desperation of relief, by any means whatever. Others were thrown into a sort of consternation, not unlike a frenzy occasioned by a raging fever; being ready to do anything or everything to obtain relief, but yet, unhappily not knowing what, when, where, how . . . But the greater part, as I conceive, though I may be mistaken in this, were firmly united in a consistent, however imprudent or desperate a plan, to run all risks, to tempt all hazards, to go all lengths, if things were driven to extremity, rather than to submit; preferring death itself to what they esteemed so wretched and inglorious a servitude.

Jonathan Mayhew, D.D., of Boston; Sermon, ''The Snare Broken,'' 1766.

TO GUARD WITH WAKEFUL ATTENTION

History affords no example of any nation, country, or people, long free, who did not take some care of themselves; and endeavor to guard and secure their own liberties. Power is of a grasping, encroaching nature, in all beings, except in Him to whom it emphatically "belongeth" . . . Power aims at extending itself, and operating according to mere will, wherever it meets with no balance, check, control, or opposition of any kind. For which reason it will always be necessary for those who would preserve and perpetuate their liberties, to guard them with a wakeful attention.

Jonathan Mayhew, D.D., of Boston; Sermon, "The Snare Broken," 1766.

EVERY UNDUE SALLY OF THE SOUL

The present state of things will afford frequent occasions of trying the virtue as well as the wisdom of rulers.—Like other men they are exposed to temptations, and perhaps to more and greater than others; and human nature at best is very imperfect. The temper of domination, so strongly interwoven in the make of man, may induce them to a wanton exercise of the power reposed in them. Flattery by its soothing addresses and artful insinuations may insensibly divert them from a right course, and lead them to dispense the blessings of government with a partial hand . . . Firmness of mind is therefore necessary to repel *these* and a thousand other temptations—to suppress every undue sally of the soul, and to urge the spring of action, that they may pursue with steadiness and vigor the great end of their office . . .

The art of self-denial must be learned and frequently practiced by them;—a prevailing attachment to their own private interests and gratifications be given up to the public—angry resentments be tempered down to the standard of right action,—their ease superseded by incessant labors, and sacrificed to the benefit of others.

Daniel Shute, A.M., of Hingham; Mass. Election Sermon, 1768.

NOT CHARITY, BUT JUSTICE

It is incumbent on a people cheerfully to support civil government. This is not to be viewed as a part of charity and generosity, but of justice. The support of those, who employ their time and talents to serve the public, should be made easy and honorable. Those who diligently attend to the duties of their stations have care, labor, and anxiety enough: People should not increase these by withholding from them an adequate reward for their services.

Jason Haven, A.M., of Dedham; Mass. Election Sermon, 1769.

NECESSITY OF CIVIL GOVERNMENT

The state of things in our world is evidently such as to render civil government necessary. But for this, life, liberty, and property would be exposed to fatal invasion.

Jason Haven, A.M., of Dedham; Mass. Election Sermon, 1769.

THE PATRIOTIC PART

It is hard to say whether this country ever has seen, or ever will see, a more important time than the present, when it seems as if the question, whether this people and all they enjoy shall be at the absolute disposal of a distant Legislature, is soon to be determined. It is not improbable, Gentlemen, that in the circle of the year, things of greatest moment may come under your consideration. If it is so determined above, may God grant you grace to act the disinterested, noble, patriotic part.

Charles Turner, A.M., of Duxbury; Mass. Election Sermon, 1773.

PRICE OF LIBERTY

While liberty is fruitful in trade, industry, wealth, learning, religion, and noblest virtue, all that is great and good and happy; slavery clogs every sublimer movement of the soul, prevents everything excellent, and introduces poverty, ignorance, vice and universal misery among a people. But if a few general terms can give no tolerable idea of the blessings of freedom, let them be learned from the story of the world; let their richness be estimated by the price that has been paid for them, in lands that have been favored with them, and particularly by our Progenitors. Heaven grant that the present generation may come by a just sense of the excellency of their civil and sacred immunities, as may be necessary for the same, at a cheaper rate, than by experience of such sufferings as our ancestors underwent.

Charles Turner, A.M., of Duxbury; Mass. Election Sermon, 1773.

REMARKABLY TENDER PEOPLE

As a people we have been remarkably tender both of our civil and religious liberties; and 'tis hoped the fervor of our regard for them will not cool till the sun shall be darkened, and the moon shall not give her light.

Gad Hitchcock, A.M., of Pembroke; Mass. Election Sermon, 1774.

THE DAY IS ARRIVED

The important day is now arrived that must determine whether we shall remain free, or, alas! be brought into bondage, after having long enjoyed the sweets of liberty. The event will probably be such as is our own conduct . . . Our trade ruined, our plantations trodden down, our cattle slain or taken away, our property plundered, our dwellings in flames, our families insulted and abused, are calamities that we are not accustomed to, and that we cannot realize but with the utmost pain; and yet we must expect more or less of these should we be compelled to betake ourselves to the sword in behalf of our rights.

William Gordon, A.M., of Roxbury; Thanksgiving Sermon, 1774.

BECAUSE WE REFUSE SUBMISSION

Our King, as if impelled by some strange fatality, is resolved to reason with us only by the roar of his cannon, and the printed arguments of muskets and bayonets. Because we refuse submission to the despotic power of a ministerial Parliament, our own sovereign, to whom we have always been ready to swear true allegiance,—whose authority we never meant to cast off,—has given us up to the rage of his Ministers, to be seized at sea by the rapacious commanders of every little sloop of war and piratical cutter, and to be plundered and massacred by land by mercenary troops, who know no distinction betwixt an enemy and a brother, between right and wrong; but only like brutal pursuers, to hunt and seize the prey pointed out by their masters.

Samuel Langdon, D.D., of Harvard College; Mass. Election Sermon, 1775.

ASSISTING THE COMMON CAUSE

There is not an individual but may be aiding and assisting to the common cause one way or other . . . The godly by their inwrought, fervent prayers, which avail much with their heavenly Father. The martial and courageous by their personal bravery. The timid by concealing their fears, withdrawing themselves whenever their fears would be apt to appear and produce a baneful influence. The poor may assist by determining that tho' poor they will be free; and that if they cannot have riches, they will not wear chains. And the rich, by the loan of their money, that so the necessary expenses may be supplied, and the defense of the country may not fall through, for want of the requisites for carrying it on. Nothing can be more faulty than for the rich to decline hazarding their cash, while exempted from hazarding their persons; nor more simple than for them, through fear of losing some of their riches, to endanger the losing them all, together with their liberties.

William Gordon, of Roxbury; Mass. Election Sermon, 1775.

WELL, THINK NOW!

The importance of this union and firmness increases day by day. For we have made opposition. The sword has been drawn, battles have been fought, and sundry fortresses have been reduced, by the forces raised by the common consent of the Colonies. Well, think now, what the consequences would probably be, if we should be overcome. Why, we should doubtless be obliged to pay all the expenses that the crown is put to in subduing us; which would take the greatest part of our estates, were we to submit, even now. But besides this, we have reason to fear that all our lands would be declared forfeit to the crown, according to the common sentence against Rebels, which they are pleased to call us.

Robert Ross, of Stratford; Sermon, "The Union of the Colonies," 1775.

ON THE NIGHT OF APRIL EIGHTEENTH

At length on the night of the eighteenth of April, 1775, the alarm is given on the hostile designs of the troops. The *militia of this town* are called together to consent and prepare for whatever might be necessary . . . In the meantime, under cover of the darkness, a brigade of these instruments of violence and tyranny, make their approach, and with a quick and silent march, on the morning of the nineteenth, they enter this town. And this is the place where the fatal scene begins! They approach with the morning light; and more like *murderers* and *cutthroats,* than the troops of a *christian king,* without provocation, without warning, when no war was proclaimed, they draw the *sword of violence,* upon the inhabitants of this town, and with a *cruelty* and *barbarity,* which would have made the most hardened savage blush, they *shed* INNOCENT BLOOD . . . Yonder field can witness the innocent blood of our brethren slain! There the tender father bled, and there the beloved son! There the hoary head and there the

blooming youth . . . They have not bled, they shall not
bleed in vain.

Jonas Clark, A.M., of Lexington; Sermon, April 19, 1776.

COUNTERFEIT SCARCITY

Blessed be God, there is a sufficiency in the land of the
necessaries of life; and if somebody is not wanting, all the
poor may be supplied. And as to many, if not most, foreign
articles of great importance, there is undoubtedly a con-
siderable supply. How then comes it to pass that such
mutual jealousies should arise, as to make an *artificial*
scarcity where we all know there is none? For God's sake,
don't let us counterfeit a scarcity lest he bring a real one!
But let town and country open their stores and their hands,
and, to the utmost of their power, supply each other.

Samuel Webster, A.M., of Salisbury; Mass. Election Sermon, 1777.

WHAT IS EXPENSE TO US?

At some seasons, when all lies at stake, it is impossible
but taxes and tribute run high. And when necessary they
should be readily paid, unless they outrun all the benefit,
which can hardly be where *property, liberty,* and *life* are
all at stake together. To talk of expence in such a case is to
dream. For 'till it be determined whether we have anything
or not, what is expense to us?

Samuel Webster, A.M., of Salisbury; Mass. Election Sermon, 1777.

CURSES OF CLOWNS

The growls of avarice and curses of clowns will generally be heard when the public liberty and safety call for

more generous and costly exertions. Indeed, we may never expect to find the marks of public virtue, the efforts of heroism, or any kind of nobleness in a man who has no idea of nobleness and excellency but what he hoards up in his barn or ties up in his purse.

Phillips Payson, A.M., of Chelsea; Mass. Election Sermon, 1778.

THIS RISING EMPIRE

Let us not amuse ourselves with a prospect of peace, and in consequence thereof abate in our preparations for the war. If we should, it may prove greatly injurious to the freedom and glory of this Rising Empire.

Samuel Stillman, A.M., of Boston; Mass. Election Sermon, 1779.

IN THAT HALLOWED PLACE

It has been said that every nation is free that deserves to be so. This may not be always true: But had a people so illuminated as the inhabitants of these states, so nurtured by their ancestors in the love of freedom; a people to whom divine Providence was pleased to present so fair an opportunity of asserting their natural right as an independent nation, and who were even compelled by the arms of their enemies to take sanctuary in the temple Liberty; had such a people been disobedient to the heavenly call, and refused to enter, who could have asserted their title to the glorious wreaths and peculiar blessings that are no where bestowed ' but in that hallowed place?

Samuel Cooper, D.D., of Boston; Mass. Election Sermon, 1780.

PEACE, BUT—

Peace, peace, we ardently wish; but not upon terms dishonorable to ourselves, or dangerous to our liberties; and our enemies seem not yet prepared to allow it upon any other. At present the voice of Providence, the call of our still invaded country, and the cry of everything dear to us, all unite to rouse us to prosecute the war with redoubled vigor . . . Amidst all our mistakes and errors, we have already done great things, but our warfare is not yet accomplished. And our rulers, we hope, like the Roman General, will think nothing done while anything remains undone.

Samuel Cooper, D.D., of Boston; Mass. Election Sermon, 1780.

ABLE MEN

By "able men" may be intended men of courage, of firmness and resolution of mind,—men that will not sink into despondency at the sight of difficulties, or desert their duty at the approach of danger,—men that will hazard their lives in defense of the public, either against internal sedition, or external enemies; that will not fear the resentment of turbulent, factious men; men that will decide seasonably upon matters of importance, and firmly abide by their decision, not wavering with every wind that blows . . .

By "able men" may be further intended men capable of enduring the burden and fatigue of government,—men that have not broken or debilitated their bodies or minds by the effeminating pleasures of luxury, intemperance, or dissipation. The supreme government of a people is always a burden of great weight, though more difficult at some times than others. It cannot be managed well without great diligence and application.

Simeon Howard, A.M., of Boston; Mass. Election Sermon, 1780.

THE ANXIOUS APPREHENSION

It is the anxious apprehension of many, that at present, we have more reason to fear misery and distress arising from that spirit of licentiousness, and that tendency to anarchy and confusion, which seems to be working in the land, than we have from our open enemies.

Moses Mather, M.A., of Middlesex; Conn. Election Sermon, 1781.

JUST RISING UP

The American states are now in their infancy, and but just rising up, and making their appearance in the world: much still remains to be done for their establishment. To this end the war must be vigorously prosecuted; the army be kept up, be suitably provided for, encouraged, and rewarded; and our enemies counteracted in all their plots and schemes . . . Good government must also be kept up among ourselves, which is the most effectual method to obtain respect, credit, and influence abroad.

Moses Mather, M.A., of Middlesex; Conn. Election Sermon, 1781.

VII

The Vindication of Liberties

WARRANTABLE AND GLORIOUS

Some have thought it warrantable and glorious to disobey the civil powers in certain circumstances, and in cases of very great and general oppression, when humble remonstrances fail of having any effect; and when the public welfare cannot be otherwise provided for and secured, to rise unanimously even against the sovereign himself, in order to redress their grievances; to vindicate their natural and legal rights; to break the yoke of tyranny, and free themselves and posterity from inglorious servitude and ruin. It is upon this principle that many royal oppressors have been driven from their thrones into banishment, and many slain by the hands of their subjects. It was upon this principle that Tarquin was expelled from Rome, and Julius Caesar, the conqueror of the world and the tyrant of his country, cut off in the senate-house. It was upon this principle that James II. was made to fly that country which he aimed at enslaving; and upon this principle was that revolution brought about which has been so fruitful of happy consequences to Great Britain.

Jonathan Mayhew, A.M., of Boston; Sermon, 1750.

UNION TO THE LATEST POSTERITY

We highly value our connection with Great Britain. There is perhaps not a man to be found among us who would wish to be independent of our mother country; we should regret the most distant thought of such an event. We are grieved that there is anything to create the least suspicion of want of tenderness on their part, or of duty on ours. We hope there is no ground for either. We trust our King and his parliament will yet hear us and confirm our liberties and immunities to us. And we earnestly pray that a happy union may subsist between Great Britain and her colonies to the latest posterity.

Andrew Eliot, A.M., of Boston; Mass. Election Sermon, 1765.

AS A BIRD FROM A SNARE

In my poor opinion, we never had so much real occasion for joy on any temporal account, as when we were thus emancipated [from the Stamp Act], and our soul escaped as a bird from a dreadful snare. And I am persuaded that it would rejoice the generous and royal heart of his majesty, if he knew that by a single turn of the scepter, when he assented to the repeal, he had given more pleasure to three million good subjects, than ever he and his royal grandfather gave them by all the triumphs of their arms, from Lake Superior eastward to the isles of Manila.

Jonathan Mayhew, D.D., of Boston; Sermon, "The Snare Broken," 1766.

NOR WERE THE JEWS MORE PLEASED

Another thing in this "news" [of the repeal of the Stamp Act], making it "good," is the hopeful prospect it gives us of being continued in the enjoyment of certain liberties and privileges, valued by us next to life itself. Such are those of being "tried by our equals" and of "making grants for the support of government of that which is our own, either in person, or by representatives we have chosen for that purpose." Whether the colonists were invested with a right to these liberties and privileges which ought not to be wrested from them, or whether they were not, 'tis the fact of truth that they really thought they were; all of them as natural heirs to it by being born subjects to the British crown, and some of them by additional charter-grants, the legality of which, instead of being contested, have all along from the days of our fathers, been assented to and allowed of by the supreme authority at home. And they imagined, whether justly or not I dispute not, that their right to the full and free enjoyment of these privileges was their righteous due, in consequence of what they and their forefathers had done and suffered in subduing and defending these American lands . . . It was eminently this that filled their minds with jealousy, and at length a settled fear, lest they should gradually be brought into a state of the most abject slavery. This it was which gave rise to the cry, which became general throughout the colonies, "We shall be made to serve as bondservants; our lives will be bitter with hard bondage." Nor were the Jews more pleased with the royal provision in their day, which, under God, delivered them from their bondage in Egypt, than were the colonists with the repeal of that act which so greatly alarmed their fears and troubled their hearts.

Charles Chauncy, D.D., of Boston; Thanksgiving Sermon, 1766.

A VERY IMPROPER SAFEGUARD

Those, who in camp, and in the field of battle, are our glory and defense; from the experience of other nations, will be thought, in time of peace, a very improper safeguard, to the constitution, which has Liberty—British Liberty, for its basis.

When a people are in subjection to those, who are detached from their fellow citizens,—under distinct laws and rules—supported in idleness and luxury—armed with the terrors of death—under the most absolute command—ready and obliged to execute the most daring orders—What must!—What has been the consequence!

Inter arma silent leges.

Samuel Cooke, A.M., of Cambridge; Mass. Election Sermon, 1770.

NOT AN INCENDIARY

I mean not, my respectable Hearers, to prove an Incendiary among you; a character under which, it seems, the Clergy of this country have been, tho' very unjustly represented by some, on the other side of the water.

Deeply penetrated as I am with a sense of liberty, and ardently in love with it; and tenderly concerned for the prosperity and happiness of my native land, I abhor a licentious and factious spirit;—I detest the baneful principle.

John Tucker, A.M., of Newbury; Mass. Election Sermon, 1771.

DEMOSTHENES AND PHOCION

Demosthenes and Phocion were both Statesmen and Eminent Orators at Athens, but men of very different tempers. Demosthenes, full of fire, often urged the people to bold and daring enterprises. Phocion, calm and sedate, persuaded to methods more practical. Meeting one day, after having harangued the people; says Demosthenes,— "These Athenians, Phocion, will murder you in some of their *mad* fits." "The same," replied Phocion, "may fall to you, if ever they come to be sober."

John Tucker, A.M., of Newbury; Mass. Election Sermon, 1771.

LOYAL AND DUTIFUL SUBJECTS

We have had the approbation of our Sovereign and of the British Parliament on several occasions in years past. And we hope the same will soon come, when it will appear that we have not done anything to forfeit either the favor of the one, or confidence of the other; but have acted the part of loyal and dutiful subjects; tho' we cannot submit to shackles and chains, so long as we have a just right to the privileges of freemen.

Moses Parsons, A.M., of Newbury Falls; Mass. Election Sermon, 1772.

AS A KIND OF ATONEMENT

It is greatly to be desired that, for the future, the ministers of our benevolent impartial Lord, may pay a due regard to liberty, as well as subjection to principalities; as a kind of atonement for the dishonor that has been reflected on the Gospel, and the immense damages done to an enslaved world by clergymen's excessive compliance to men in power.

Charles Turner, A.M., of Duxbury; Mass. Election Sermon, 1773.

TO STAND FAST IN LIBERTY

For men to stand fast in their liberty means, in general, resisting the attempts that are made against it, in the best and most effectual manner they can.

When anyone's liberty is attacked or threatened, he is first to try gentle methods for his safety; to reason with, and persuade the adversary to desist, if there be opportunity for it; or get out of his way if he can; and if by such means he can prevent the injury, he is to use no other.

But the experience of all ages has shown that those, who are so unreasonable as to form designs of injuring others, are seldom to be diverted from their purpose by argument and persuasion alone.

Simeon Howard, A.M., of Boston; Artillery Election Sermon, 1773.

ONLY DEFENSIVE WAR

It is only defensive war that can be justified in the sight of God. When no injury is offered us, we have no right to molest others. And Christian meekness, patience, and forbearance are duties that ought to be practiced by kingdoms and individuals.

Simeon Howard, A.M., of Boston; Artillery Election Sermon, 1773.

WHEN THE PARENT STATE CONTENDS

It must be acknowledged, America never saw a day so alarming as the present. The unhappy controversy which now subsists between Great Britain and these Colonies, is more painful than any of the distressing wars we have formerly been engaged in. When the savages annoyed our infant settlements, or those whom we used to consider as *natural enemies* threatened to invade us, duty and interest pointed us to the means of safety. Our young men offered themselves freely . . .

But when the parent state is contending with us, nothing but the *last* extremity, nothing but the preservation of *life,* or that which is of more importance, LIBERTY, can ever prevail with us to make resistance.

John Lathrop, A.M., of Boston; Thanksgiving Sermon, 1774.

AMERICANS HAVE BEEN USED TO WAR

Americans who have been used to war from their infancy, would spill their best blood, rather than *"submit to be hewers of wood, or drawers of water, for any ministry or nation in the world."*

But we hope in God, and it shall be our daily prayer, that matters may never come to this. We hope some wise and equitable plan of accommodation may take place. For the salvation of the parent state, as well as of these provinces, we sincerely hope the measures, with respect to America, adopted by the *last* Parliament, and pursued with vigor by the ministry, may be essentially altered by *this*.

John Lathrop, A.M., of Boston; Thanksgiving Sermon, 1774.

NOT ABOUT TRIFLES

Our danger is not visionary, but real. Our contention is not about trifles, but about liberty and property. And not ours only, but those of posterity to the latest generations. And every lover of mankind will allow that these are important objects, too inestimably precious and valuable enjoyments to be treated with neglect and tamely surrendered.

Gad Hitchcock, A.M., of Pembroke; Mass. Election Sermon, 1774.

PAID VERY DEAR

The people in this province, and in the other colonies, love and revere civil government—they love peace and order—but they are not willing to part with any of those rights and privileges for which they have, in many respects, paid very dear.

Gad Hitchcock, A.M., of Pembroke; Mass. Election Sermon, 1774.

IF THE GREAT SERVANTS FORGET

If the great servants of the public forget their duty, betray their trust, and sell their country, or make war against the most valuable rights and privileges of the people, reason and justice· require that they should be discarded, and others appointed in their room, without any regard to formal resignations of their forfeited power.

Samuel Langdon, D.D., of Harvard College; Mass. Election Sermon, 1775.

WHO ARE THE JUDGES?

If it be asked, "Who are the proper judges to determine when rulers are guilty of tyranny and oppression?" I answer, the public. Not a few disaffected individuals, but the collective body of the state, must decide this question; for, as it is the collective body that invests rulers with their power and authority, so it is the collective body that has the sole right of their institution or not. Great regard ought always to be paid to the judgment of the public. It is true the public may be imposed upon by a misrepresentation of facts; but this may be said of the public, which cannot always be said of individuals, viz., that the public is always willing to be rightly informed, and when it has proper matter of conviction laid before it, its judgment is always right.

Samuel West, A.M., of Dartmouth; Mass. Election Sermon, 1776.

NOT UNNOTICED

Injustice, oppression, and violence (much less the shedding of innocent blood) shall not pass unnoticed by the just Governor of the world. Sooner or later, a just recompense will be made upon such workers of iniquity.

Jonas Clark, A.M., of Lexington; Sermon April 19, 1776.

THIS BOTTOMLESS GULF

Tyrants always support themselves with standing armies! And if possible the people are disarmed. . . . When it comes to this, it is extremely difficult for them to unite in sufficient bodies to effect their deliverance. But if they would *unite,* nothing, nothing, could stand before them. So that in a word the *want of union, the want of union,* is the ruin of the world. For want of this those noble spirits who would risque all to be free, are forced to sit down in chains!

When therefore we see in a manner the whole world, except these American states, groaning under the most abject slavery, with so few successful attempts to deliver themselves, how stupid must we be, if we do not exert ourselves, to the utmost to save ourselves from falling into this remediless estate, this bottomless gulf of misery.

Samuel Webster, A.M., of Salisbury; Mass. Election Sermon, 1777.

A HAPPY OMEN

A spirit of union is certainly a most happy omen in a state, and upon righteous principles should be cultivated and improved with diligence. It greatly strengthens public measures, and gives them vigor and dispatch; so that but small states when united, have done wonders in defending their liberties against powerful monarchs. Of this we have a memorable example in the little state of Athens, which destroyed the fleet of Xerxes, consisting of a thousand warships, and drove Darius with his army of three hundred thousand men out of Greece.

Phillips Payson, A.M., of Chelsea; Mass. Election Sermon, 1778.

NOT POWER BUT FREEDOM

We are engaged in a most important contest; not for *power* but *freedom.* We mean not to change our masters, but to secure to ourselves, and to generations, yet unborn, the perpetual enjoyment of civil and religious liberty, in their fullest extent.

Samuel Stillman, A.M., of Boston; Mass. Election Sermon, 1779.

MOST VIGOROUS EFFORTS

Such as are inimical and treacherous to our freedom have acted very different parts in the present day. Some have acted an open part, and have gone and joined the enemy; while others have chosen still to continue at home among us; who have been much more hurtful to us, and helpful to the enemy, than those who have gone off and openly joined them. They, many of them, maintain a secret correspondence with the enemy, give them intelligence, carry on a clandestine trade with them. . . . Every argument therefore, which will justify us in our opposition to Great Britain, strongly pleads for our most vigorous efforts to detect, and make examples of such secret enemies as endeavor to conceal themselves among us.

Moses Mather, M.A., of Middlesex; Conn. Election Sermon, 1781.

'TIS DONE! 'TIS DONE!

'Tis done! 'tis done! Our work is done: our warfare is accomplished; our inestimable rights are established on a sure foundation.

John Lathrop, A.M., of Boston; "Discourse on the Peace," 1784.

VIII

The Obligations of Liberty

THE USE WE MAKE OF THEM

Though we are not an independent state, yet, Heaven be thanked! we are a free people. However, all know that it is not from our privileges and liberties, simply considered, but from the use we make of them, that our felicity is to be expected.

Jonathan Mayhew, D.D., of Boston; Mass. Election Sermon, 1754.

TO THE HIGHEST BIDDER

People have in some countries been so regardless of their own welfare, as to give too much encouragement to designing men, who would practice upon them; yea, as to make an infamous merchandise of their hands and voices to the highest bidder.

Jonathan Mayhew, D.D., of Boston; Mass. Election Sermon, 1754.

THE GOSPEL AND RULERS

'Tis certain that the gospel, above all other religions, instructs mankind in the duties they owe unto their lawful rulers.

Edward Dorr, A.M., of Hartford; Conn. Election Sermon, 1765.

A PEOPLE MAY BE DECEIVED

A people may be deceived, they may be betrayed by men in whom they put confidence. But they deserve to be abandoned by providence if they trust their interest with men whom they know to be either weak or wicked.

Andrew Eliot, A.M., of Boston; Mass. Election Sermon, 1765.

WE ARE INDULGED

We may now be easy in our minds—contented with our condition. We may be at peace and quiet among ourselves, everyone minding his own business. All ground of complaint that we are "sold for bond-men and bond-women" is removed away, and, instead of being slaves to those who treat us with rigor, we are indulged the full exercise of those liberties which have been transmitted to us as the richest inheritance from our forefathers. We have now greater reason than ever to love, honor, and obey our gracious king, and pay all becoming reverence and respect to his two Houses of Parliament; and may with entire confidence rely on their wisdom, lenity, kindness, and power to promote our welfare.

Charles Chauncy, D.D., of Boston; Sermon on the Repeal of the Stamp Act, 1766.

CHRISTIANITY AND PATRIOTISM

Is Christianity inconsistent with patriotism? God forbid that any should imagine such a thing. The true Christian is the best qualified to act the part of the patriot, if he hath other qualifications also which are requisite.

Ebenezer Bridge, A.M., of Chelmsford; Mass. Election Sermon, 1767.

LET BRITAIN LEARN SOBERLY

Britain, most highly favored of God in the preservation of her civil and religious freedom, while most of the neighbor nations have been enslaved to despotic power and arbitrary sway; and the tyranny of prelates, as well as princes. Let her rejoice herein, and learn soberly and virtuously to use both her power and her liberty, which will thus be, as it has been, her glory and her safety.

Richard Salter, A.M., of Mansfield; Conn. Election Sermon, 1768.

AS IN THE SOLAR SYSTEM

As in a well constituted civil state there is a subordination among rulers, and each has his respective part to act with a view to the general good; so to carry the grand design into execution it is necessary that each should keep the line of his own particular department; every eccentric motion will introduce disorder and be productive of mischief: but each keeping a steady and regular course in his own sphere, will dispense a benign influence upon the community, and harmoniously conspire to promote the general good: As in the solar system, every planet revolving in its own orbit round the sun produces that order and harmony which secures the conservation of the whole.

Daniel Shute, A.M., of Hingham; Mass. Election Sermon, 1768.

ONE GRAND POINT

The cause in which rulers and ruled are engaged is the same, though the parts they have to act are different; *these* all tend to one grand point, the welfare of the community; and people are as much obliged to fidelity and ardor in the discharge of their duty, as rulers to theirs, in supporting the common cause.

Daniel Shute, A.M., of Hingham; Mass. Election Sermon, 1768.

BY THE BOUNTY OF THE CREATOR

Though in the constitution of things it does not belong to man to live alone, or without government in society; yet he is invested with certain rights and privileges, by the bounty of the Creator, so adapted to his nature that the enjoyment of them is the source of his happiness in this world, and without which existence here would not be desirable. And mankind have no right voluntarily to give up to others those natural privileges, essential to their happiness, with which they are invested by the Lord of all: for the improvement of *these* they are accountable to Him.

Daniel Shute, A.M., of Hingham; Mass. Election Sermon, 1768.

ETHIOPIA HAS LONG STRETCHED OUT HER HAND

I trust on this occasion I may without offense plead the cause of our African slaves, and humbly protest the pursuit of some effectual measures at least to prevent the future importation of them. Difficulties insuperable, I apprehend, prevent an adequate remedy for what is past. Let the time pass wherein we, the patrons of liberty, have dishonored the Christian name, and degraded human nature nearly to the level of the beasts that perish. Ethiopia has long stretched out her hands to us. Let not sordid gain, acquired by the merchandise of slaves and the souls of men, harden our hearts against her piteous moans. When God ariseth, and when he visiteth, what shall we answer? May it be the glory of this province, of this respectable General Assembly, and, we could wish, of this session, to lead in the cause of the oppressed.

Samuel Cooke, A.M., of Cambridge; Sermon on "The True Principles of Civil Government," 1770.

ACT AS FREE!

Let us act as *free!* Let us stand up for our just rights; but consider ourselves at the same time as servants of God, and submit to every ordinance of man for the Lord's sake. Let us never use our liberty for a cloak of maliciousness.

John Tucker, A.M., of Newbury; Mass. Election Sermon, 1771.

EQUALLY BOUND

Proper submission in a free state is a medium between slavish subjection to arbitrary claims of rulers, on the one hand, and a lawless license, on the other. It is obedience in subjects to all orders of government, which are consistent with their constitutional rights and privileges. So much submission is due, and to be readily yielded by every subject; and beyond this, it cannot be justly demanded, because Rulers and People are equally bound by the fundamental laws of the constitution.

The state of the world, and temper of mankind, may render these observations necessary and highly important;—important and necessary as a check upon Rulers of a despotic turn; and a restraint upon the licentious among the people; that neither, by breaking over their just bounds, may disturb the peace, and injure the happiness of the state.

John Tucker, A.M., of Newbury; Mass. Election Sermon, 1771.

PRIVILEGE AND DUTY

The people ought to have the end of government, the public good, at heart, as well as the magistrate; and therefore to yield all loyal subjection to well regulated government, in opposition to everything of a factious nature and complexion. And for the same reason, it is not only their privilege, but it is also their duty, properly to assert their freedom, and take all rational and necessary methods for the public security and happiness, when constitutional boundaries are broken over, and so their rights are invaded.

Charles Turner, A.M., of Duxbury; Mass. Election Sermon, 1773.

FOREIGN TO GOD'S DESIGN

That the civil ruler and Christian minister should engross the wealth of the world to themselves, as they have done in many countries and ages, and live in pride and luxury, on spoils violently extorted, or slily drained from the people, is altogether foreign to the design of God in setting them up. It is His mind that both, acting in character, should be reverenced and honorably provided for; but His grand view, in raising them to their places of eminence, is, that the one should *do good* in religious, the other in civil respects, to the world.

Charles Turner, A.M., of Duxbury; Mass. Election Sermon, 1773.

OUR DUTY TOWARD THIS UNION

It is our duty, as we love righteousness,—as we love peace,—as we love our country,—as we love the parent state,—ourselves and millions of unborn posterity, it is our duty to do all in our power to strengthen and perpetuate *this union*. And was I not sure you are ready even of yourselves, I would urge you, my friends and fellow citizens, by arguments which influence my own mind, ''to abide by and strictly adhere to the *Resolutions* of the Continental Congress, as the most peaceable and probable method of preventing confusion and bloodshed, and of restoring that harmony between Great Britain and these colonies.''

John Lathrop, A.M., of Boston; Thanksgiving Sermon, 1774.

BOUND TO OBEY

When a people have by their free consent conferred upon a number of men a power to rule and govern them, they are bound to obey them. Hence disobedience becomes a breach of faith; it is violating a constitution of their own appointing, and breaking a compact for which they ought to have the most sacred regard. Such a conduct discovers so base and disingenuous a temper of mind, that it must expose them to contempt in the judgment of all the sober, thinking part of mankind.

Samuel West, A.M., of Dartmouth; Mass. Election Sermon, 1776.

WHILE NOBLY OPPOSING

But while we are nobly opposing with our lives and estates, the tyranny of the British Parliament, let us not forget the duty which we owe to our lawful magistrates; let us never mistake licentiousness for liberty. The more we understand the principles of liberty, the more readily shall we yield obedience to lawful authority; for no man can oppose good government but he that is a stranger to true liberty . . . It is with peculiar pleasure that I reflect upon the peaceable behavior of my countrymen at a time when the courts of justice were stopped and the execution of laws suspended. It will certainly be expected of a people that could behave so well, when they had nothing to restrain them but the laws written in their hearts, that they will yield all ready and cheerful obedience to lawful authority.

Samuel West, A.M., of Dartmouth; Mass. Election Sermon, 1776.

JUST A HINT

Just a hint to the people of some things which seem to me most likely to guard against tyranny in their rulers:

Let the people by all means encourage schools and colleges, and all the means of learning knowledge.

Let them do all in their power to suppress vice and promote religion and virtue.

Let only men of *integrity* be entrusted by you with any power.

Let not too much power be trusted in the hands of any.

Let elections of the Legislators be frequent; and let bribery and corruption be guarded against to the utmost.

Let the militia be kept under the best regulation, and be made respectable.

Let standing armies be only for necessity and for a limited time.

Let these armies never be put under the absolute power of any magistrate in time of peace, so as to act in any cause, till that cause is approved by the Senate and the people.

Let monopolies and all kinds and degrees of oppression be carefully guarded against.

Finally, Let the powers and prerogatives of the rulers and the rights and privileges of the people be determined with as much precision as possible, that all may know their limits. And where there is any dispute, let nothing be done, till it is settled by the people, who are the fountain of power.

Samuel Webster, A.M., Salisbury; Mass. Election Sermon, 1777.

THE PUBLIC STILL CALLS

The public still calls aloud for the united efforts both of rulers and people; nor have we as yet put off the harness. We have many things amiss among ourselves that need to be reformed,—many internal diseases to cure, and secret internal enemies to watch against . . . We wish for much greater exertions to promote education, and knowledge, and virtue, and piety. But in all states there will be such as want no learning, no government, no religion at all.

Phillips Payson, A.M., of Chelsea; Mass. Election Sermon, 1778.

ANIMATION AND PASSION

Would to God that the animation of piety was as strong and universal as the passion for liberty.

Chauncey Whittelsey, A.M., of New Haven; Conn. Election Sermon, 1778.

THE FREE-BORN AFRICANS

In order to complete a system of government and to be consistent with ourselves, it appears to me that we ought to banish from among us that cruel practice, which has long prevailed, of reducing to a state of slavery for life, the free-born Africans.

The Deity hath bestowed upon them and us the same natural rights as men; and hath assigned to them a part of the globe for their residence. But mankind, urged by those passions which debase the human mind, have pursued them to their native country; and by fomenting wars among them, that they might secure the prisoners, or employing villains to decoy the unwary, have filled their ships with the unfortunate captives; dragged them from their tenderest connections, and transported them to different parts of the earth, to be hewers of wood and drawers of water, till death shall end their painful captivity.

To reconcile this nefarious traffic with reason, humanity, religion, or the principles of a free government, in my view, requires an uncommon address . . .

May the year of jubilee soon arrive when Africa shall cast the look of gratitude to these happy regions for the TOTAL EMANCIPATION OF HER SONS!

Samuel Stillman, A.M., of Boston; Mass. Election Sermon, 1779.

TO ANIMATE THE MACHINE

When a people have the rare felicity of choosing their own government, every part of it should first be weighed in the balance of reason, and nicely adjusted to the claims of liberty, equity and order. But when this is done, a warm and passionate patriotism should be added to the result of cool deliberation, to put in motion and animate the whole machine.

Samuel Cooper, D.D., of Boston; Sermon preached before Governor John Hancock, the Senate and House of Massachusetts on October 25, 1780, "being the day of the commencement of the Constitution and inauguration of the new Government."

DOUBTLESS TASTE THE SWEETS

We have at present a happy constitution of government, framed by wise men and accepted by a majority of people at large. If we adhere to the spirit of it, and labor to give energy to the laws, and dignity to the governing authority, by electing *wise men and true,* and then submitting cheerfully to their commands, we shall doubtless taste the sweets of that liberty for which we have bled at every vein.

Zabdiel Adams, A.M., of Lunenburgh; Sermon preached at Lexington on April 19, 1783.

NOT ENOUGH TO BE FREE

My brethren, it is not enough that we be free and independent; it is not enough that we have liberty of conscience, and advantages of a civil and religious nature, superior to the inhabitants of any other part of the world; we must be *wise* and *virtuous,* we must be governed by that religion which we profess, we must be influenced by those doctrines which we say we believe, as we hope to be a happy people.

John Lathrop, A.M., of Boston; "Discourse on the Peace," 1784.

IX

Types of Liberty

Civil Liberty
Freedom Through Education
Religious Liberty

Civil Liberty

TWO THINGS IN GENERAL

We may very safely assert these two things in general, without undermining government: One is, that no civil rulers are to be obeyed when they enjoin things that are inconsistent with the commands of God. All such disobedience is lawful and glorious . . . Another thing that may be asserted with equal truth and safety is, that no government is to be submitted to at the expense of that which is the sole end of all government—the common good and safety of society . . . The only reason of the instituting of civil government, and the only rational ground of submission to it, is the common safety and utility.

Jonathan Mayhew, A.M., of Boston; Sermon, 1750.

WHO ARE THE MORE CRIMINAL?

It is not easy to determine who are the more criminal,— they who would make their way to places of power and trust by indirect means, or they who have so little concern for the welfare of their country as to hearken to them.

Jonathan Mayhew, D.D., of Boston; Mass. Election Sermon, 1754.

CRAMP, ENFEEBLE, AND DIMINISH

Persecution and intolerance are not only unjust and criminal in the sight of God, but they also cramp, enfeeble, and diminish the state.

Jonathan Mayhew, D.D., of Boston; Mass. Election Sermon, 1754.

THE FREEST GOVERNMENTS

Civil liberty is in the greatest perfection, and those are the freest governments, where, on the one hand, the sovereign is secured from tyranny and an abuse of power, and the people from anarchy, confusion, and disobedience.

Benjamin Stevens, A.M., Kittery; Mass. Election Sermon, 1761.

NURSING FATHERS

The practice of religion and virtue tends, above all things, to promote the public welfare and happiness of mankind, and to secure the ends of civil government; therefore rulers should be nursing fathers to it. Civil government was originally instituted to protect and defend men's lives and liberties, to guard and secure their properties, and promote their temporal interests and advantages

. . . Now the practice of religion and virtue, tends, above all other things, to promote those very ends, for which men entered into society.

Edward Dorr, A.M., of Hartford; Conn. Election Sermon, 1765.

WHAT A RESOURCE!

If the repeal of this [Stamp] Act should be the means of continuing our religious as well as civil liberties, and of transmitting pure and undefiled religion to future ages: Oh! What a resource will it be of perpetual and everlasting praises!

Nathaniel Appleton, M.A., of Cambridge; Thanksgiving Sermon, 1766.

GOOD LAWS

Laws may be said to be good, when they are such as tend to the promoting of the good of the society, and of individuals in it—or, they are good, when they tend to the securing and establishing the liberties and privileges of men; which they are entitled unto, by the constitution of the government they have voluntarily engaged to submit to; and which are confirmed to them by the revealed will of God.

And I will add here, that only such laws as these, are fit for the government of rational, intelligent, moral agents, all equal and upon a par, antecedent to any political combinations among men; and after all, entitled to certain immunities and benefits, as members of the body politic.

Ebenezer Bridge, A.M., of Chelmsford; Mass. Election Sermon, 1767.

THIS AUSPICIOUS DAY

The return of *this day* [Election of the Council] is auspicious to our civil liberties, and fills every honest heart with joy. The liberty of choosing men from among ourselves, whose interest is inseparably connected with the *whole,* for his Majesty's Council in the province, whose part is not only to aid the power of legislation, but also "freely to give advice at all times to the Governor for the good management of the public affairs of government," will always be considered as a privilege *dear* and *sacred* by all who are not, by blind prejudice or sordid views, lost to a sense of the inestimable value of their natural and constitutional freedom.

Daniel Shute, A.M., of Hingham; Mass. Election Sermon, 1768.

NOT A RESIGNATION

Civil government among mankind is not a resignation of their natural privileges, but that method of securing them.

Daniel Shute, A.M., of Hingham; Mass. Election Sermon, 1768.

A READY COMPLIANCE

With indifference to surrender constitutional rights, or with rashness to oppose constitutional measures, is equally to *rebel* against the state. Anarchy and slavery are both diametrically opposite to the genius of the British constitution, and indeed to the constitution of the God of nature; and equal care at least is to be taken to avoid the former as the latter. A ready compliance with constitutional measures will always justify a tenacious claim to constitutional privileges, and support the hope of their continuance.

Daniel Shute, A.M., of Hingham; Mass. Election Sermon, 1768.

GENERALLY EXPLODED

Men have the natural right to determine for themselves, in what way, and by whom they will be governed. The notion of a divine, indefeasible right to govern, vested in particular persons or families, is wholly without foundation; and is, I think, as generally exploded at this day, by men of sober minds, as that of uninterrupted succession in ecclesiastical office.

Jason Haven, A.M., of Dedham; Mass. Election Sermon, 1769.

THE BENEFITS OF THE CONSTITUTION

Fidelity to the public requires that the laws be as plain and explicit as possible, that the less knowing may understand, and not be ensnared by them, while the artful evade their force. Mysteries of law and government may be made a cloak of unrighteousness. The benefits of the constitution and of the laws must extend to every branch and each individual in society, of whatever degree, that every man may enjoy his property, and pursue his honest course of life with security. The just ruler is sensible in trust for the public, and with an impartial hand will supply the various offices in society . . . He will not, without sufficient reason, multiply lucrative offices in the community, which naturally tends to introduce idleness and oppression. Justice requires that the emoluments of every office, constituted for the common interest, be proportioned to their dignity and the services performed for the public; parsimony, in this case, enervates the force of government, and frustrates the most patriotic measures. A people, therefore, for their own security, must be supposed willing to pay tribute to whom it is due, and freely support the dignity of those under whose protection they confide. On the other hand, the people may apprehend that they have just reason to complain of oppression and wrong, and to be jealous of their liberties, when subordinate public offices are made the surest step to wealth and ease.

Samuel Cooke, A.M., of Cambridge; Mass. Election Sermon, 1770.

JOINT PILLARS

A free state will no longer continue unless the constitution is maintained entire in all its branches and connections. If the several members of the legislative power become entirely independent of each other, it produceth a schism in the body politic; and the effect is the same when the executive is in no degree under the control of the legislative power,—the balance is destroyed, and the execution of the laws left to arbitrary will. The several branches of civil power, as joint pillars, each bearing its due proposition, are the support, and the only proper support, of a political structure regularly formed. A constitution which cannot support its own weight must fall.

Samuel Cooke, A.M., of Cambridge; Mass. Election Sermon, 1770.

A DECENT FREEDOM OF SPEECH

The just ruler will not fear to have his public conduct critically inspected, but will choose to recommend himself to the approbation of every man. As he expects to be obeyed for conscience' sake, he will require nothing inconsistent with its dictates, and be desirous that the most scrupulous mind may acquiesce in the justice of his rule. As in his whole administration, so in this, he will be ambitious to imitate the supreme Ruler, who appeals to his people—"Are not my ways equal?" Knowing, therefore, that his conduct will bear the light, and his public character be established by being fully known, he will rather encourage than discountenance a decent freedom of speech, not only in public assemblies, but among the people. This liberty is essential to a free constitution, and the ruler's surest guide.

Samuel Cooke, A.M., of Cambridge; Mass. Election Sermon, 1770.

TO GUARD AGAINST EXTREMES

My reverend fathers and brethren in the ministry will remember that it is part of the work and business of a gospel minister to teach his hearers the duty they owe to magistrates. Let us, then, endeavor to explain the nature of their duty faithfully, and show them the difference between liberty and licentiousness; and, while we are animating them to oppose tyranny and arbitrary power, let us inculcate upon them the duty of yielding due obedience to lawful authority. In order to the right and faithful discharge of this part of our ministry, it is necessary that we should thoroughly study the law of nature, the rights of mankind, and the reciprocal duties of governors and governed. By this means we shall be able to guard them against the extremes of slavish submission to tyrants on the one hand, and of sedition and licentiousness on the other.

Samuel West, A.M., of Dartmouth; Mass. Election Sermon, 1776.

THE TRUE DESIGN OF GOVERNMENT

The true design of civil government is to protect men in the enjoyment of liberty.

Samuel West, A.M., of Dartmouth; Mass. Election Sermon, 1776.

THE GREATEST OF ALL BLESSINGS

Religious or spiritual liberty must be accounted the greatest happiness of man, considered in a private capacity. But considering ourselves here as connected in civil society, and members one of another, we must in this view esteem civil liberty as the greatest of all human blessings. This admits of different degrees, nearly proportioned to the morals, capacity, and principles of a people, and the mode of government they adopt; for, like the enjoyment of other blessings, it supposes an aptitude or taste in the possessor. Hence a people formed upon the morals and principles of the gospel are capacitated to enjoy the highest degree of civil liberty, and will really enjoy it, unless prevented by force or fraud.

Phillips Payson, A.M., of Chelsea; Mass. Election Sermon, 1778.

FULL LIBERTY OF THE PRESS

The full liberty of the press—that eminent instrument of

promoting knowledge, and great palladium of the public liberty—being enjoyed, the learned professions directed to the public good, the great principles of legislation and government, the great examples and truths of history, the maxims of generous and upright policy, and the severer truths of philosophy investigated and apprehended by a general application to books, and by observation and experiment,—are means by which the capacity of a state will be strong and respectable, and the number of superior minds will be daily increasing . . . The variety and freedom of opinion is apt to check the union of a free state; and in case the union be interrupted merely from the freedom of opinion, contesting for real rights and privileges, the state and its government may still be strong and secure, as was the case in ancient Rome, in the more disinterested periods of that republic. But if parties and factions, arising from false ambition, avarice, or revenge, run high, they endanger the state, which was the case in the latter periods of the republic of Rome. Hence the parties in a free state, if aimed at the public liberty and welfare, are salutary; but if selfish interest and views are their source, they are both dangerous and destructive.

Samuel West, A.M., of Dartmouth; Mass. Election Sermon, 1778.

SACRED REGARD

I desire to bless God that, in my youth, I was taught to pay a sacred regard to the rights of mankind. The design of civil government, I was taught, is to secure life, personal freedom, liberty of conscience, and that property which men acquire by lawful means.

John Lathrop, A.M., of Boston; "Discourse of the Peace," 1784.

Freedom Through Education

LEARNING AND GOVERNMENT

Suffer me to recommend the College [Yale] to your protection. The interests of learning are so nearly connected with the good of Government, that the Legislature, I trust, will think it an object worthy of your attention.

Stephen White, of Windham; Conn. Election Sermon, 1763.

LEARNING AS NURSE AND OFFSPRING

Learning is another great and inestimable blessing to society . . . Imagination can scarce paint the superior condition of that state, where learning, science, and the liberal arts flourish, to that of a rude and unpolished people . . . Learning is both the nurse and offspring of public-spirit.

Noah Welles, A.M., of Stamford; Conn. General Assembly Sermon, 1763.

GOVERNMENT AND SCIENCE

Knowledge and learning may well be considered as most essentially requisite to a free, righteous government. A republican government and science mutually promote and support each other. . . .

Every kind of useful knowledge will be carefully encouraged and promoted by the rulers of a free state, unless they should happen to be men of ignorance themselves, in which case they and the community will be in danger of sharing the fate of blind guides, and their followers. The instruction of youth by instructors properly qualified, the establishment of societies for useful arts and sciences, the encouragement of persons of superior abilities will always command the attention of wise rulers.

The late times of our glorious struggle have not indeed been favorable to the cause of education in general; though much useful knowledge of the geography of our country, of the science of arms, of our abilities and strength, and of our natural rights and liberties, has been acquired; great improvements and discoveries have also been made in several kinds of manufactory. But our security and the public welfare requires yet greater exertions to promote education and useful knowledge.

Phillips Payson, A.M., of Chelsea; Mass. Election Sermon, 1778.

GREATER EXERTIONS FOR EDUCATION

As nothing will be omitted that the good of the state calls for, we expect to see greater exertions in promoting the means of education and knowledge than ever have been made among us. You will especially allow me, my fathers, to recommend our college [Harvard], so much the glory of our land, to your special attention and most generous encouragements; for everything that is excellent and good that we hope and wish for in future, in a most important and essential sense, is connected with and depends upon exertions and endeavors of this kind.

Phillips Payson, A.M., of Chelsea; Mass. Election Sermon, 1778.

NEITHER PIETY, VIRTUE, OR LIBERTY

Neither piety, virtue, or liberty can long flourish in a community where the education of youth is neglected. . . . The sciences and arts, for the encouragement of which a new foundation [The American Academy of Arts and Sciences] hath lately been laid in this Commonwealth, deserve the countenance and particular favor of every government. They are not only ornamental but useful. They not only polish, but support, enrich, and defend a community. As they delight in liberty, they are particularly friendly to free states.

Samuel Cooper, D.D., of Boston; Mass. Election Sermon, 1780.

LIBERTY AND LEARNING

Liberty and learning are so friendly to each other, and so naturally thrive and flourish together, that we may justly expect that the guardians of the former will not neglect the latter. The good education of children is a matter of great importance to the commonwealth. Youth is the time to plant the mind with the principles of virtue, truth, and honor, the love of liberty and of their country, and to furnish it with all useful knowledge; and though in this business much depends upon parents, guardians, and masters, yet it is incumbent upon the government to make provision for schools and all suitable means of instruction.

Simeon Howard, A.M., of Boston; Mass. Election Sermon, 1780.

LITERATURE AND THE PUBLIC WELFARE

The cultivation of literature will greatly promote the

public welfare. In every community, while provision is made that all should be taught to read the scriptures, and the very useful parts of common education, a good proportion should be carried through the higher branches of literature. Effectual measures should be taken for preserving and diffusing knowledge among a people. The voluntary institution of libraries in different vicinities will give those who have not a liberal education an opportunity of gaining that knowledge which will qualify them for usefulness. Travels, biography, and history, the knowledge of the policies, jurisprudence, and scientific improvements among all nations, ancient and modern, will form the civilian, the judge, the senator, the patrician, the man of useful eminence in society. The colleges have been of singular advantage in the present day. When Britain withdrew all her wisdom from America, this revolution found above two thousand, in New England only, who had been educated in the colleges. . . . It would be for the public emolument should there always be found a sufficient number of men in the community at large of vast and profound erudition, and perfect acquaintance with the whole system of public affairs, to illuminate the public councils, as well as to fill the three learned professions with dignity and honor.

Ezra Stiles, D.D., President of Yale College; Conn. Election Sermon, 1783.

Religious Liberty

SUCKLED WITH HUMAN BLOOD

The interest of true religion has been greatly prejudiced

by that notion which has so generally prevailed in Christendom from the days of Constantine. I mean that kings could not be *nursing fathers,* nor queens *nursing mothers* to the Church, unless they suckled her with human blood, and fed her with the flesh of those whom angry Ecclesiasticks are pleased to stigmatize with the names of heretic, schismatic, and infidel.

Jonathan Mayhew, D.D., of Boston; Mass. Election Sermon, 1754.

LAWS OF A PERSECUTING ASPECT

It may be worth considering whether we have not some laws in force, hardly reconcilable with that religious liberty which we profess . . . A neighboring colony, we know, has lately been reprimanded on account of some laws of a persecuting aspect. And whether some of our own are of a genius and complexion sufficiently abhorrent from the same spirit, is not perhaps unworthy the consideration of the legislature.

Jonathan Mayhew, D.D., of Boston; Mass. Election Sermon, 1754.

RELIGIOUS LIBERTY SUPPOSES

Religious liberty supposes that there be not only free inquiry, but equal freedom of profession and action, when thereby no disturbance is given to others.

Benjamin Stevens, A.M., of Kittery; Mass. Election Sermon, 1761.

UTTER STRANGERS

To Gallic slavery, to Romish persecution and spiritual

bondage, (blessed be God) we are utter strangers. Still we taste the dear, the delightful sweets of liberty.

Noah Welles, A.M., of Stamford; Conn. General Assembly Sermon, 1764.

OUR HIGHLY FAVORED NATION

As to religion, and religious liberties and privileges, what people in the whole world are so highly favored as our nation? We have the gospel, the freest use and the fullest enjoyment of it . . . No menaces from the civil power to compel men in matters of religion; no impositions from authorized ecclesiastical tyrants; no persecution for religious sentiments or practices.

Ebenezer Bridge, A.M., of Chelmsford; Mass. Election Sermon, 1767.

RELIGIOUS RIGHTS AND HAPPINESS

On the free exercise of their natural religious rights the present as well as future happiness of mankind greatly depends.

Daniel Shute, A.M., of Hingham; Mass. Election Sermon, 1768.

IF ONE FALLS

Religious liberty is so blended with civil, that if one falls it is not to be expected that the other will continue.

Charles Turner, A.M., of Duxbury; Mass. Election Sermon, 1773.

LIBERTY OF PRIVATE JUDGMENT

There are some natural liberties or rights which no person can divest himself of, without transgressing the law of nature. A man cannot, for instance, give up the liberty of private judgment in matters of religion, or convey to others a right to determine of what religion he shall be, and in what way he shall worship God. A grant of this nature would destroy the foundation of all religion in the man who made it, and must be a violation of the law of nature.

Simeon Howard, A.M., of Boston; Artillery Election Sermon, 1773.

THE PIOUS RULER AND THE PUBLIC GOOD

The greatest restraints, the noblest motives, and the best supports arise from our holy religion. The pious ruler is by far the most likely to promote the public good. His example will have the most happy influence; his public devotions will not only be acts of worship and homage to God, but also of charity to men. Superior to base passions and little resentments, undismayed by danger, not awed by threatenings, he guides the helm in storm and tempest, and is ready, if called in providence, to sacrifice his life for his country's good. Most of all concerned to approve himself to his God, he avoids the subtle arts of chicanery, which are productive of so much mischief in a state; exercising a conscience void of offense, he has food to eat that the world knows not of.

Phillips Payson, A.M., of Chelsea; Mass. Election Sermon, 1778.

ALL PROTECTED; NONE ESTABLISHED

For though Christians may contend among themselves about their religious differences, they will all unite to promote the good of the community, because it is their interest, so long as they all enjoy the blessings of a free, and equal administration of government.

On the other hand, if the magistrate destroys the equality of the subjects of the state on account of religion, he violates a fundamental principle of a free government, establishes separate interests in it, and lays a foundation for disaffection to rulers, and endless quarrels among the people.

Happy are the inhabitants of that commonwealth . . . in which all are *protected,* but none *established!*

Samuel Stillman, A.M., of Boston; Mass. Election Sermon, 1779.

HAPPY UNION OF ALL DENOMINATIONS

I know there is a diversity of sentiment respecting the extent of civil power in religious matters. Instead of entering into the dispute, may I be allowed from the warmth of my heart to recommend, where conscience is pleaded on both sides, mutual candor and love, and a happy union of all denominations in support of a government, which though human, and therefore not absolutely perfect, is yet certainly founded on the broadest basis of liberty, and affords equal protection to all. Warm parties upon civil or religious matters, or from personal considerations, are greatly injurious to a free state, and particularly so to one newly formed. We have indeed less of this than might be expected: we shall be happy to have none at all.

Samuel Cooper, D.D., of Boston; Mass. Election Sermon, 1780.

RIGHTS OF CONSCIENCE

No man who has full liberty of inquiring and examining for himself, of openly publishing and professing his religious sentiments, and of worshiping God in the time and manner which he chooses, without being obliged to make any religious profession or attend any religious worship contrary to his sentiments, can justly complain that his rights of conscience are infringed. And such liberty and freedom every man may enjoy, though the government should require him to pay his proportion toward supporting public teachers of religion and morality.

Simeon Howard, A.M., of Boston; Mass. Election Sermon, 1780.

DEPURATED FROM RUST AND CORRUPTION

And while Europe and Asia may hereafter learn that the most liberal principles of law and civil polity are to be found on this side of the Atlantic, they may also find the true religion here depurated from the rust and corruption of ages, and learn from us to reform and restore the church to its primitive purity. It will be long before the ecclesiastical pride of the splendid European hierarchies can submit to learn wisdom from those whom they have been inured to look upon with sovereign contempt. But candid and liberal disquisition will, sooner or later, have a great effect. Removed from the embarrassments of corrupt systems, and the dignities and blinding opulence connected with them, the unfettered mind can think with a noble enlargement, and with an unbounded freedom, go wherever the light of truth directs. Here there will be no bloody tribunals, no cardinal's inquisitors-general, to bend the human mind, forcibly to control the understanding, and to put out the light of reason, the candle of the Lord in Man,—to force an innocent Galileo to renounce truths demonstrable as the light of day. Religion may here receive its last, most liberal, and impartial examination. Religious liberty is peculiarly friendly to fair and generous disquisition.

Ezra Stiles, D.D., Sermon on "The Future Glory of the United States," Hartford, 1783.

X

America the Free

FROM THIS REMARKABLE DAY

From this *remarkable day* will an important *era* begin for both *America* and *Britain*. And from the *nineteenth of April,* 1775, we may venture to predict, will be dated in future history, THE LIBERTY or SLAVERY of the AMERICAN WORLD.

Jonas Clark, A.M., Lexington; Sermon, April 19, 1776.

HAIL, MY HAPPY COUNTRY!

To anticipate the future glory of America from present hopes and prospects is ravishing and transporting to the mind. In this light we behold our country, beyond the reach of all oppressors, under the great charter of independence, enjoying the purest liberty; beautiful and strong in its union; the envy of tyrants and devils, but the delight of God and all good men; a refuge to the oppressed; the joy

of the earth . . . Hail, my happy country, saved of the
Lord! Happy land, emerged from the deluges of the Old
World, drowned in luxury and lewd excess! Hail, happy
posterity, that shall reap the peaceful fruits of our sufferings, fatigues, and wars! With such prospects, such
transporting views, it is difficult to keep the passions or the
tongue within the bounds of Christian moderation.

Phillips Payson, A.M., of Chelsea; Mass. Election Sermon, 1778.

WITH EXTENDED VIEWS

It is laudable to lay the foundations of our Republicks
with extended views. Rome rose to empire because she
early thought herself destined for it. The great object was
continually before the eyes of her sons . . . They did great
things because they believed themselves capable, and born
to do them. They reverenced themselves and their country;
and animated with unbounded respect for it, they every
day added to its strength and glory. Conquest is not indeed
the aim of these rising states; sound policy must ever forbid
it. We have before us an object more truly great and
honorable. We seem called by heaven to make a large
portion of this globe a seat of knowledge and liberty, of
agriculture, commerce, and arts, and what is more important than all, of Christian piety and virtue . . . Our
mountains, our rivers and lakes have a singular air of
dignity and grandeur. May our conduct correspond to the
face of our country! At present an immense part of it lies as
nature hath left it. It remains for us and our posterity to

"make the wilderness become a fruitful field and the desert blossom as the rose."

Samuel Cooper, D.D., of Boston; Mass. Election Sermon, 1780.

RESERVED FOR AMERICA

All the forms of civil polity have been tried by mankind, except one, and that seems to have been reserved in Providence to be realized in America. Most of the states, of all ages, in their originals, both as to policy and property, have been founded in rapacity, usurpation, and injustice. . . . It has really been very indifferent to the great cause of right and liberty which of the belligerent powers prevailed,—a Tangrolipix or a Mahomet, an Augustus or an Antony, a Scipio or a Hannibal, a Brennus or an Antiochus,—tyranny being the sure portion of the plebians, be the victory as it should happen. . . .

Liberty, civil and religious, has sweet and attractive charms. The enjoyment of this, with property, has filled the English settlers in America with a most amazing spirit which has operated, and still will operate, with great energy. Never before has the experiment been so effectually tried of every man's reaping the fruits of his labor and feeling his share in the aggregate system of power.

Ezra Stiles, D.D., of Yale College; Conn. Election Sermon, 1783.

A GREAT, A VERY GREAT NATION

This will be a great, a very great nation, nearly equal to half Europe. Already has our colonization extended down the Ohio, and to Koskaseah on the Mississippi. And if the present ratio of increase should be rather diminished in some of the other settlements, yet an accelerated multiplication will attend our general propagation, and overspread the whole territory westward for ages. So that before the millennium the English settlements in America may become more numerous millions than that greatest dominion on earth, the Chinese Empire . . .

I am sensible some will consider these as visionary, utopian ideas; and so they would have judged had they lived in the apostolic age, and had been told that by the time of Constantine the Empire would have become Christian. As visionary that the twenty thousand souls which first settled New England should be multiplied to near a million in a century and a half. . . . As utopian would it have been to the loyalists at the battle of Lexington, that in less than eight years the independence and sovereignty of the United States should be acknowledged by four European sovereignties, one of which should be Britain herself. How wonderful the revolutions, the events of Providence! We live in an age of wonders; we have lived an age in a few years; we have seen more wonders accomplished in eight years than are usually unfolded in a century.

Ezra Stiles, D.D., of Yale College; Conn. Election Sermon, 1783.

FIGURE TO YOURSELVES

Figure to yourselves what a country this may be, if nothing out of the common course of things should happen to obstruct population for one century, from the present time. If we have now but three millions of inhabitants, in twenty-five years we may have six, in fifty years we may have twelve, in seventy-five years we may have twenty-four, in a hundred years forty-eight millions of people.

This natural increase, besides the large addition which may be expected by emigrations from the crowded parts of Europe, will not only fill up many large trading and manufacturing cities, but furnish multitudes to carry on navigation, and multitudes to penetrate the yet unexplored wilderness, and settle towns on the great rivers and lakes toward the setting sun.

Our country is divided and intersected in almost every direction, with deep waters, while a seacoast, the whole extent from east to west, gives the several states an easy communication with each other, and every advantage for navigation at large.

Favored with general peace, these states, if they continue united, *must* rise to vast importance.

John Lathrop, A.M., of Boston; "Discourse on the Peace," 1784.

Index to Ministers

This book was photo set in the Times Roman series of type. The face was designed to be used in the news columns of the *London Times*. The *Times* was seeking a type face that would be condensed enough to accommodate a substantial number of words per column without sacrificing readability and still have an attractive, contemporary appearance. This design was an immediate success. It is used in many periodicals throughout the world and is one of the most popular text faces presently in use for book work.

This book is printed on 70-pound long-fibre, acid-free paper especially developed by the S. D. Warren Company to meet the historical document standards of the United States National Historical Publications and Records Commission.

Book design by Design Center, Inc., Indianapolis, Indiana
Typography by Wichita Graphic Arts Center, Wichita, Kansas
Printed by North Central Publishing Co., St. Paul, Minnesota